Rattler!

CHRIS MATTISON

Rattler!

A NATURAL HISTORY OF RATTLESNAKES

BLANDFORD

First published 1998 in the United Kingdom by
Blandford
A Cassell Imprint
Wellington House, 125 Strand, London WC2R 0BB

Previously published in hardback 1996

Distributed in the United States by
Sterling Publishing Co., Inc.
387 Park Avenue South, New York,
NY 10016–8810

**A Cataloguing-in-Publication Data entry for this
title is available from the British Library**

ISBN 0 7137 2731 4

Designed by Richard Carr
Typeset by Litho Link Ltd, Welshpool, Powys, Wales
Printed and bound in Spain by Bookprint

Pages 2–3: Crotalus ruber lucasensis,
San Lucas rattlesnake.

CONTENTS

ACKNOWLEDGEMENTS

Several people have provided direct help with the writing and illustrating of this book and it gives me great pleasure to acknowledge their contributions. David Barker provided excellent photographs of a number of species of rattlesnakes that would not otherwise have been illustrated, as did John Tashjian. For various reasons, some of my own photographs were taken of captive snakes: Lee Buncher, Wayne Murphy, Ian Ramsden, Bradley Winfield and the staff of The Vivarium, London, all loaned or located captive specimens for me to photograph.

Wherever possible, rattlesnakes were photographed in the field: during several visits to the United States and Mexico in search of rattlesnakes and other reptiles various people have been generous with help and, perhaps more importantly, have provided good company. They include, in alphabetical order, Bob Applegate, Gretchen Davison, Lee Grismer, Eric Gergus, Brad Hollingsworth, my son James Mattison, Eric Mellink, Bill Montgomery and Humberto Wong, but there were many others whose contributions may have been smaller but are still appreciated. I apologize for not naming all of them. Lee Grismer has also been especially generous in sharing his knowledge of the rattlesnakes of Baja California and in making available information of the distribution of island forms, some of which has not yet been published. Gretchen Davison read the manuscript and made many astute and useful suggestions.

At Blandford Audrey Aitken, Jane Birch and Miranda Stonor all contributed to the accuracy of the text, while Stuart Booth was instrumental in getting the book under way.

INTRODUCTION

Rattlesnakes form a branch of the viper family – about 30 species of snakes that have evolved a unique appendage on the end of their tail. They all live in America but they have close relatives in Asia.

Along with the cobras and the boa constrictor they are probably the snakes that most capture people's imaginations, even those who are not otherwise interested in snakes. Everyone has a strong opinion about them, although very few will ever see one in the wild. Many people spend their lives avoiding the places where these snakes live. Others would like to see them exterminated altogether and some seem to spend most of their spare time trying to ensure that this will happen sooner rather than later! But most of us, I think, have a sneaking admiration for them, and we are drawn to them at zoos and side-shows just as we are drawn to the other predators – the big cats, hawks, eagles and sharks. The twin emotions of fear and fascination combine to form a potent mixture that can be hard to resist.

Although they are much smaller than us, they can deal out death in the blink of an eye. If they hunted us with the same vigour as we have hunted them, the American countryside would be a very dangerous place. Fortunately, they prefer to avoid confrontation whenever possible by hiding, fleeing or warning us of their deadly presence. What other creature has the apparatus to cause a rapid and gruesome death at one end but uses it in anger only if the equipment at the other end fails to have the desired effect?

No wonder that a large number of myths, legends and old wives' tales has built up around rattlesnakes. Some of the stories are more credible than others, but together they form an important part of the folklore of the places where they live, especially the American West.

Rattlesnakes are also special to biologists because they represent the very pinnacle of reptilian evolution. They are the most up-to-date snakes – state of the art. They have features and accessories that are not found in other models – if they were motor cars or dishwashers everybody would want one!

Despite their high profile and their evolutionary importance, how much do we really know about rattlesnakes? What makes them tick?

The most frequently asked questions are factual ones – How big? How dangerous? How many? – and we must try to answer these questions. Frankly, though, there is little true natural history in these dry statistics. Saying that such and such a species grows to about 120cm (4ft) in length gives no impression of its presence when it glides across the desert; the fact that most species 'eat rodents' gives no picture of the superbly adapted hunting and killing machine that is the essence of a rattlesnake. When we say that the colour of this or that species matches its surroundings, how can we hope to convey the seemingly magical way in which it escaped our notice until we almost trod on it? And, as our foot hit the ground and the snake sounded off, our rush of adrenalin owed nothing whatsoever to the fact that the rattle oscillated at about 50 cycles a second.

Biological facts should be taken for what they are – the raw material of natural history. Raw material, by itself, is of little use unless we use it to make something more valuable – a better understanding of plants and animals, of the ways in which they live and of the forces that have shaped them. But the story of evolution is incomplete – we do not have *all* the facts, and perhaps we never will. We have to speculate a little, take a leap into the unknown, be prepared to adjust our conclusions from time to time. This is what natural history should be about. Rather than present only the known facts about rattlesnakes, I have tried to capture some of their spirit, to imagine what it must be like to be a rattlesnake. I hope that this book will provide answers to some of the questions about them but, equally important, it should also encourage a greater respect for them.

We can never solve all the mysteries of nature. It is partly for this reason that we cannot afford to plunder and abuse it. The American environmentalist Aldo Leopold said: 'The first rule of intelligent tinkering is to keep all the parts.' This includes the rattlesnakes.

The Santa Catalina Island 'rattleless' rattlesnake, Crotalus catalinensis.

1

THE RATTLERS

Rattlesnakes belong to the family of snakes known as the vipers or Viperidae. More specifically, they belong to the subdivision of vipers known as pit vipers. There are 206 species of vipers, of which 138 are pit vipers; 30 of these are rattlesnakes.

Rattlesnakes have a very characteristic appearance. This is most obvious in the tail department! Apart from their rattle, though, they have certain other shared features, such as general body shape. In some respects, such as colour and markings, the species differ noticeably from one another; sometimes, there are even differences between populations of the same species and, if these are constant enough, they may be classified as subspecies.

Size

To the layman, one of the most interesting things about a snake is its size, and this is often the subject of much speculation and exaggeration. 'How big do rattlesnakes grow?' is a question to which there are several answers – if you asked ten people who knew about snakes you would probably get ten different answers. Part of the discrepancy would be due to the way in which they would interpret the concept of 'maximum size' – some would be concerned with the size to which a given species will normally grow, whereas others may cite the lengths of abnormally large specimens.

Over the years this kind of misunderstanding, together with some fairly 'creative' measuring, has caused endless confusion and controversy, but the huge lengths claimed in the past for rattlesnakes have now been more or less dismissed in favour of more modest, verifiable records. It must also be said that estimating the length of snakes in the wild is quite difficult – they rarely stretch themselves out for long enough to allow accurate measurements to be taken. (There is also a tendency for the large one that got away to grow even larger in the imagination, as with fish!)

Crotalus ruber lorenzoensis, *San Lorenzo rattlesnake.*

So, how large *do* they grow? Taking length first, most experts consider that the eastern diamondback (*Crotalus adamanteus*) is the longest species. Large adults can measure up to 1.8m (nearly 6ft) and the largest that was reliably measured was just over 2.4m (a shade under 8ft). The average size of this species, however, is probably somewhere around 1.2–1.4m (4–5ft).

The next longest species is probably the western diamondback (*C. atrox*), which can very occasionally grow to more than 2m (6ft 6in) and has been recorded up to 2.13m (almost 6ft 11in). Again, though, the average size of an adult of this species is probably closer to 1m (3ft 3in), or very slightly more.

Third in our league table comes the neotropical rattlesnake (*C. durissus*), some forms of which can also grow to slightly over 2m (6ft 6in) in exceptional circumstances (such as in captivity) but which usually reaches a maximum size of about 1.5m (5ft) and an average of just above 1m (3ft 3in).

These figures might seem disappointingly low compared with the fanciful reports of ten-foot rattlesnakes that were made earlier this century. Remember, though, that even a four-foot rattler is a large and impressive beast when seen face to face, and an angry six-footer must be truly awesome. Furthermore, rattlesnakes are quite heavy-bodied when compared with other types of snakes, with a specimen of 1.5m (5ft) weighing in at about 2kg (4½lb) and one of 2m (6ft 6in) weighing over 5kg (just over 11lb). Few other snakes, except the large boas and pythons, exceed 5kg (11lb), and it is likely that no other venomous snakes even approach this weight except the Central and South American bushmaster and, perhaps, the largest African viper, the Gaboon viper, which normally grows to about 1.2m (4ft).

Apart from the three rattlesnakes mentioned above, there are a number of others that one can loosely describe as 'large'. The timber and canebrake rattlesnakes, the red diamond rattlesnake, the Mojave and certain forms of the western rattlesnake have all been recorded at over 1m (3ft 3in) long. The 'giant' population of speckled rattlesnakes on the island of Angel de la Guarda, in the Gulf of California, can also grow to over 1m (3ft 3in) in length, although the species is not normally large.

We can think of 'medium-sized' rattlesnakes as those that do not quite reach a metre in length and that average around 0.5–0.75m (20–30in). They include the black-tailed rattlesnake and the tiger rattlesnake, but there are plenty of others. Similarly, there are numerous small species (including many of the montane rattlesnakes and the pygmy rattlesnakes, *Sistrurus*) that only occasionally grow to more than 0.5m (20in). All of these species are described in Chapter 5, with a note of their approximate size.

Regardless of the average size of the species, the largest individuals are nearly always males. The evolutionary reasons for this are discussed on page 68. The only known exception is that of the sidewinder, in which females are, on average, longer than males.

Shape

Compared with other snakes in North America, rattlers are among the most heavy-bodied. In Central and South America, however, they are up against serious opposition where size is concerned in the form of several large boas and other pit vipers. In their body proportions, or shapes, the 30 species are rather similar to each other; variation due to the age, sex and general condition of each individual tends to obscure what little differences there may be between species. The sidewinder is a notable exception because it is consistently heavier (and therefore thicker) than any of the other species for which figures are available. Perhaps its unique habitat preference and its method of locomotion have a bearing on this.

The sexes also vary in shape, even after allowing for other factors. Female rattlesnakes are proportionately thicker than males of the same species, as in most other snakes, and this difference represents a weight difference of about 20 per cent more than males of approximately the same length. As with other figures of this kind, there is a great deal of variation, and factors such as the condition of the snakes must be taken into account.

SIZE AND SHAPE OF THE HEAD

Rattlesnakes' heads are characteristically wide and roughly spade-shaped. The great width of the head is necessary to accommodate the venom glands, which are located just behind the eyes (other vipers also share this characteristic). They have rounded snouts when viewed from above, but this is more apparent in some species than in others. When the size of the head is compared with that of the body, there is a general trend for small species of rattlesnakes to have relatively larger heads than large species. Similarly, young rattlesnakes have relatively larger heads than adults of the same species (as in almost all animals). Certain species deviate from the general pattern but, with a couple of exceptions, this is very slight and only apparent when one takes accurate measurements. The exceptions are the speckled rattlesnake (*Crotalus mitchellii*) and, especially, the tiger rattlesnake (*C. tigris*), which both have noticeably small heads. The eastern diamondback (*C. adamanteus*) has a proportionately larger head than other species of the same size but this difference is slight and not obvious from casual observation.

Variations in the shape of the head are slight, except for the differences in the arrangement of the head scales between members of the genera *Crotalus* and *Sistrurus* (see page 20). The ridge-nosed rattlesnake (*Crotalus willardi*) is well named; in profile, it has a prominent ridge running around the top of its snout, from eye to eye. Other species, such as the Baja rattlesnake (*C. enyo*) and the lance-headed rattlesnake (*C. polystictus*), have narrower than average heads, while others, like the speckled rattlesnake (*C. mitchellii*) and the sidewinder (*C. cerastes*), have wider than average heads. The latter two species also have unusually flattened heads when compared with other rattlers (Fig. 1). These small differences, however, do not detract from the general statement that rattlesnakes are, collectively, a fairly uniform group of snakes.

In keeping with this, rattlesnakes do not have the same variety of ornamentation that one finds in some other vipers, which may take the form of soft fleshy horns on the snout (in several European vipers belonging to the genus *Vipera*) or spiny scales above the eyes (in several African species such as the horned adder, *Bitis caudalis*, and the South American eyelash viper, *Bothriechis schlegelii*). The closest that any rattlesnake gets to this sort of ornamentation is the raised scales above the eyes (the supraocular scales) of sidewinders.

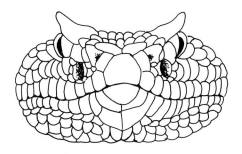 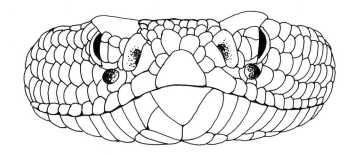

Fig. 1 *The sidewinder,* Crotalus cerastes *(left), is the only species with prominent raised scales (supraoculars) over its eyes. The head of the speckled rattlesnake,* Crotalus mitchellii *(right), is flatter than most other rattlesnakes.*

TAIL LENGTH

Rattlesnakes have relatively short tails and two explanations have been proposed. Firstly, all stout-bodied snakes tend to have short tails because a long tail would serve no useful purpose to them – the snakes that need long tails are those that are fast-moving or those that use them for climbing. Rattlesnakes do not fall into either of these categories. Secondly, it may be easier for the snake to vibrate its rattle when it is at the end of a short tail rather than a long one. Having said this, however, there is no reason why a rattlesnake with a long tail could not vibrate just its tip. Even so, it is a fact that, with few exceptions, the rattlesnakes with the longest tails are also the ones with the smallest rattles – the long-tailed rattlesnake (*Crotalus stejnegeri*) and the pygmy rattlesnake (*Sistrurus miliarius*) are examples.

Colour and pattern

Colour and pattern are important to snakes as well as to snake watchers. From the snake's point of view, its colour and markings help it to remain undetected while it rests, basks or lies in ambush for its food – how well it does these things can mean the difference between life and death. For the watcher, each snake's colour and markings help to identify it. Unfortunately many species of rattlesnakes are similar to each other when seen at a safe distance, and identification is made even harder by the tendency for many species to occur in a number of different colours. Because they rely on camouflage, snakes from the same locality will have similar coloration, even if they belong to different species. Conversely, if a single, wide-ranging species occurs in places that have different coloured soils or rocks its colour will vary from one population to the next.

Males and females are similarly coloured in all the species of rattlesnakes except two. These are the banded rock rattlesnake (*Crotalus lepidus*), in which males are often greenish-grey (with black crossbars) compared with the plain grey background colour of females, and a subspecies of the Mexican dusky rattlesnake, *C. triseriatus armstrongi*, in which females are brown or greyish while males have a greenish or yellowish cast. Nobody knows why the sexes are different in these rattlesnakes or, for that matter, why such differences are not found in other species.

Taking rattlesnakes as a whole, then, the most common colours are 'earthy' ones: browns, greys, yellowish-greys, greenish-greys and reddish-browns. There are no brightly coloured rattlesnakes, although some captives may seem fairly conspicuous if they are displayed on an alien background.

As in other animals, the colours are produced by pigments. The cells containing the pigment are called chromatophores, and they can be subdivided according to the type of pigment they contain. The chromatophores most commonly found in rattlesnakes are melanophores, producing black or brown colours, and guanophores, producing white or cream. Other chromatophores produce reds, yellows and blues but these are nearly always overlaid with a sprinkling of melanophores, resulting in muted colours. If one examines the scales closely, however, the individual specks of many different colours are visible. The snake's markings are produced by the way in which the chromatophores, especially the melanophores, are scattered and distributed over its body.

Broadly speaking, rattlesnakes' patterns can be divided into the following categories: diamond-backed, blotched, spotted, banded and plain, of which the first two are the most common. Some snakes have markings that are intermediate between two categories (e.g. diamonds and blotches), while in others blotches on the neck and back tend to become crossbars further down towards the tail. The

Opposite: *Like several rattlesnakes, the red diamond rattler,* Crotalus ruber, *has bold black and white bands on its tail.*

Below: *Eye stripes feature quite commonly in a variety of rattlesnake species. The way in which these disguise the position and shape of the eye can be seen to good effect in the eastern diamondback,* Crotalus adamanteus.

markings of some species and subspecies are obscured by pigment and are difficult to see clearly. It can be especially hard to make out the markings of a rattlesnake that is about to shed its skin.

One marking that is fairly constant within the group is the stripe that runs from somewhere near the eye to somewhere near the angle of the jaw. This is the ocular stripe, and it may be dark in colour with paler borders, or pale in colour surrounded by darker areas. Whichever way round the colours are, the function of the stripe is certainly to disguise the whereabouts of the snake's eye. Being bright and rounded, eyes are hard to camouflage and can easily give away an animal's presence. It is common for animals that rely on camouflage to have stripes passing through or near their eyes.

Another common marking, seen in several species, is the black and white banding around the tail, immediately in front of the rattle. Although we usually associate this with the western diamondback, the Mojave, red diamond and western rattlesnakes also have it, although it is not always so obvious. The black-tailed rattlesnake, of course, has a black tail and some other species, especially the canebrake rattlesnake, tend to become darker towards their tails.

Although variation in colour and markings is natural and can be expected within any population of animals, occasional individuals crop up that are very different from the other members of their species. These aberrant individuals arise through genetic accidents and are unlikely to occur in great numbers in any given population except under unusual circumstances. A number of colour variations occur in rattlesnakes, of which albinism and melanism are the two most obvious. In albinism, all pigmentation is lacking and so the snake appears white (or nearly so) with pink eyes. Melanism has the opposite effect: a superabundance of black pigmentation obscures all the other markings and the snake is black in colour.

There are quite a few records of albino rattlesnakes, although they do not seem to be as frequent as they are in some other snake genera. Usually, albino specimens are juvenile. Being poorly camouflaged they are unlikely to live to a ripe old age under natural conditions and, in addition, albinos often have poor eyesight (although this is likely to be less of a drawback for a rattlesnake, with their other well-developed senses, than for most other animals). In captivity, albinos may live as long as normally coloured individuals and, if they reproduce, they can lead to a colony of albino snakes after a couple of generations.

Melanism does not always have such a drastic effect as albinism. To start with, albinism tends to be an all or nothing condition,

Albinos have been recorded in a number of rattlesnake species. This is a young western diamondback, Crotalus atrox.

whereas melanism varies in degree, with some snakes tending to be more melanistic than others. Under certain conditions, melanism can actually be an advantage. For instance, dark snakes warm up more quickly than light coloured ones and, in cool climates, this may give them a better chance of survival. The situation is not quite as simple as this, however. Dark coloured snakes are not usually as well camouflaged as normally coloured ones and so there is a 'trade-off' between being good at warming up and being good at avoiding predators. Natural selection will 'decide' (in the evolutionary sense) whether the advantages of warming up quickly outweigh the advantages of avoiding predators.

We would expect dark individuals to have the edge at high latitudes and in mountains, where it is cooler. Sure enough, the rattlesnake populations in which one finds black or very dark individuals are northern ones. There are examples among eastern massassaugas (*Sistrurus catenatus catenatus*) and timber rattlesnakes (*Crotalus horridus horridus*), for instance. Both these species range up into the cooler parts of north-eastern United States, and it is in the more northerly parts of their respective ranges that dark individuals are most likely to be found.

Scales

Rattlesnakes are, of course, covered in scales, but the scales are not exactly the same on every part of the snake's body: different types of scales occur in different places. The exact number and arrangement of the scales, especially on the head, can be useful in helping to identify snakes. Unfortunately, in order to study the scales of living rattlesnakes, it is necessary to become rather more intimate with them than most people are willing to be.

Each scale is formed from a thickened part of the snake's skin. This is different from fishes' scales, which are separate from the skin and quite loosely attached to it (and therefore easily detached by scraping). The head scales on most rattlesnakes are small and rather granular in appearance. In the three pygmy rattlesnakes (*Sistrurus*), however, the head scales consist of a set of nine large plates between the eyes and over the snout; these set them apart from other rattlesnakes and make them relatively easy to recognize (Fig. 2).

The more distinctive head scales, found on all rattlesnakes, include the rostral scale at the tip of the snout. This scale is typically as high as, or higher than, it is wide (when looking at the snake head on) and roughly triangular or shield-shaped. It has a notch in its

Fig. 2 *The three* Sistrurus *species have nine large plates on top of their heads (left), whereas the heads of the* Crotalus *species (right) are covered with many small irregular scales.*

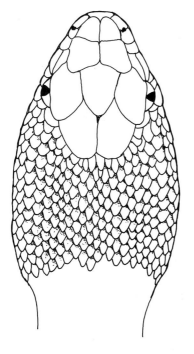
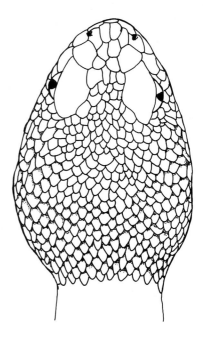

lower edge through which the snake pokes its tongue. The large scales over the eyes are called supraocular scales. They are noteworthy in many species because they may be slightly raised, as in the sidewinder, or they may have a bold and distinctive stripe across them, as in the Baja rattlesnake. Each of the snake's nostrils is situated in the nasal scale, which is sometimes divided into the prenasal and the postnasal scales (in front of and behind the nostril respectively). Finally, the scales bordering the mouth have special names – the upper and lower labials. The other head scales tend to be small and of little interest except to specialists.

Each of the scales mentioned has its own distinct shape, but the scales on the snake's body and tail are more uniform. Those on the back and sides, the dorsal scales, are pointed and have broad bases. Down the centre of each of these scales is a low ridge or keel, found in all rattlesnakes and in many other kinds of snakes. The scales on the flanks have lower keels than those on the centre of the back. The scales on the underside, the ventral scales, are different from those on the back: they are wide, have no keels and are arranged as a single row. The scales under the tail are similar but are called the subcaudals. Subcaudal scales may be single or they may be arranged in pairs. Those of rattlesnakes (and other vipers) often include some

The body scales of rattlesnakes have a ridge or keel running down their centre. Also visible on these scales of a canebrake rattler, Crotalus horridus atricaudatus, are the scattered specks of pigment that help to give the snake its colour and markings.

of each but they are normally single towards the base of the tail. Most other North American snakes have paired subcaudals. Males usually have more subcaudal scales than females of the same species, because their tails are longer.

The skin between the scales is thinner and is known as interstitial skin. Scales usually cover it completely, but when the snake swallows a large meal, for instance, it stretches and becomes visible, especially in the neck region. In rattlesnakes, though not in all snakes, it is of roughly the same coloration as the scales.

SKIN SHEDDING

Rattlesnakes are like other snakes in that they shed their skin from time to time. Snakes shed only the outer layer, called the epidermis – this is a thin, transparent layer that is supple when it first comes away but soon becomes brittle. Baby rattlesnakes always shed between seven and ten days after they are born; in juveniles, shedding may take place up to seven times each year. Adults shed only two or three times a year on average. The first shed is nearly always in the spring when the snake emerges from hibernation, while subsequent sheddings can take place at any time of the year.

The blue cast over the eyes of this northern Pacific rattlesnake, Crotalus viridis oreganus, *and its dull coloration, are indications that it will shed its skin soon.*

The whole process begins when a new epidermal layer is formed underneath the old one. About one week before shedding, the snake secretes a layer of oil between the new and old epidermal layers, its markings become dull and obscure and its eyes take on a bluish cast. About four days later, the eyes clear, and shedding occurs two or three days after this. The snake starts by rubbing its nose against a rough object to free the skin around its jaws. Once it has done this the snake crawls over rocks or among vegetation so that the old skin snags and is pulled free of its body. Eventually, the entire skin comes away and the snake leaves it behind, inside out. Rattlesnakes differ from other snakes in not shedding the skin that covers the scale at the tip of the tail.

The rattle

The small rattle of a massassauga, Sistrurus catenatus.

The rattle is, of course, the structure that sets rattlesnakes apart from all other snakes: nothing like it is found anywhere else. It consists of a series of horny shells, or segments, which fit loosely inside one another and which are made of keratin, the same material that forms animal hair, horns, claws and finger nails.

THE STRUCTURE OF THE RATTLE

Each segment of a rattle originates from the scale covering the tip of the rattlesnake's tail. In other snakes, the tail tip would be tapered and the horny epidermis covering it would be a hollow cone. Every time the snake shed its skin, the cone would come away easily with the rest. In rattlers, however, the tip of the tail has a constriction running right around it. This prevents the horny covering from coming away with the rest of the skin and so it is retained, as a segment of the rattle (Fig. 3). The snake adds another segment to the rattle each time it sheds.

In time, the rattle loses its end segments due to wear and tear. The number of segments in a wild rattlesnake rarely exceeds 12, and 5 to 10 is more usual: the record appears to be 23, but this is exceptional. Captive snakes do not seem to be subjected to the same rough and tumble as wild ones, and because of this their rattles often grow longer, the record being 29 segments. Older accounts that maintained that the age of a rattlesnake could be told by counting the segments were wrong. Young snakes may shed two to four times in a single year, while old ones may only shed once, twice or, occasionally, not at all. In addition, once the end of the rattle has broken off it is impossible to tell how many segments it has lost.

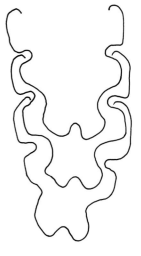

Fig. 3 *The rattle in cross section. Each segment grips the one in front of it.*

The rattle from a western diamondback rattlesnake, Crotalus atrox. *This string contains six segments; it has lost some of the older segments from its tip and so the button is missing.*

Each segment is a complicated structure. When the snake holds its rattle in the normal (i.e. resting) position, it is higher than it is wide. About halfway up each side is a shallow groove so that in cross-section it looks something like an hour-glass. The segments are not exactly symmetrical but are cunningly designed to allow for more movement in the vertical plane than in the horizontal – in other words, the segments move more when the rattle is shaken up and down than when it is shaken from side to side. Furthermore, their shape allows the rattle to curve upwards but not downwards, presumably to stop it from dragging along the ground when the snake moves (Fig. 4). When a rattler 'sounds off', it raises its tail to a vertical position and shakes it back and forth.

The shape of the rattle as a whole, as opposed to each segment, depends entirely on the number of segments and the age of the snake. Young snakes start life with a slightly swollen tip to their tail. This swelling is called the pre-button and the young snake loses it when it first sheds its skin, usually within a week or so of being born.

Fig. 4 *The rattle segments are asymmetrical so that the string can be bent upwards but will not hang down and drag along the ground when the snake moves.*

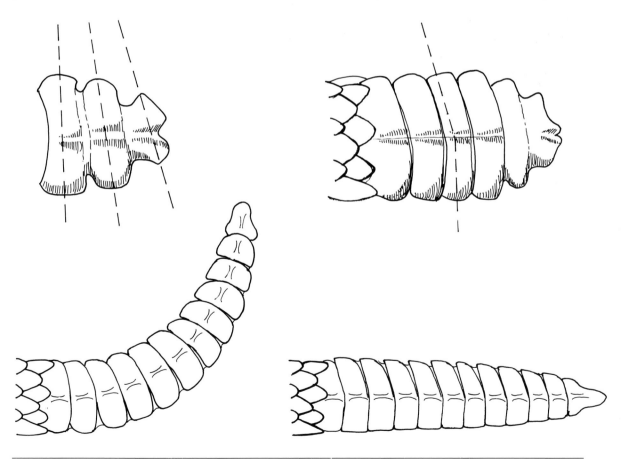

The pre-button is replaced, after shedding, with a button. This differs from the pre-button because it has a shallow constriction about halfway along its length. Because the young snake grows quickly at first, each segment is significantly larger than the one before, so the rattle becomes tapered, with the broadest segments (the most recent ones) nearest the snake's tail. As the snake approaches its eventual adult size its growth rate slows down, so that each segment is the same diameter, or only slightly larger, than the ones that went before it. By this time, the rattle will almost certainly have lost the early segments, which gave it its tapered shape, and its sides will become more or less parallel.

This juvenile timber rattlesnake, Crotalus horridus horridus, *has no rattle, only a button, showing that it has shed its skin only once.*

HOW THE RATTLE IS FORMED

Visualizing how the segments fit together is not as difficult as understanding how each one arises and how it joins the rattle string. This is best explained as a series of stages:

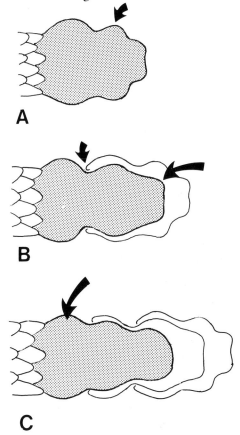

1. *As the snake approaches the time when it will shed its skin (pre-shed), the horny layer covering the scale at the end of its tail becomes thickened (Fig. 5A).*

2. *When the snake sheds, this horny layer cannot be completely discarded because of the constriction (Fig. 5B) and remains loosely in place over the end of the tail – it has now become a segment. The tip shrinks slightly, away from the inside of the old 'shell', and forms a new horny covering.*

3. *At the same time as the new tip is forming its horny layer, the part of the tail immediately in front of the rattle swells and becomes bulbous (Fig. 5C), in effect pushing the rattle (all the previous segments) further back, away from the scaly part of the tail. Now stage 1 is repeated.*

The net result of this sequence is that a new segment is added to the base of the rattle every time the snake sheds, and the old segments move along.

The senses

Rattlesnakes have an armoury of senses that enable them to interact with their surroundings. Some of them, such as their eyes, are common to most other animals, and some, such as the Jacobson's organ, are unique to snakes and lizards. One of them, the heat pit, is unique to rattlesnakes and their closest relatives, the pit vipers.

The eyes

Snakes' eyes are much simpler structures than those of most other vertebrates and are less efficient. Those of all rattlesnakes have vertically arranged pupils and this indicates that they are primarily nocturnal in their habits – nocturnal animals in other groups, such as cats, also have vertical pupils. In darkness the pupils open up and may appear round, but in daylight they contract to a slit or an ellipse. The colour of the iris usually matches that of the stripe that passes through the eye. This is often black (so the pupil is hard to pick out) but in species that lack the eye stripe it can be lighter, to match the general coloration of the snake's head. The tiger rattlesnake (*C. tigris*), for instance, has pinkish coloured irises, and those of the rock rattlesnake (*C. lepidus*) are grey.

The tongue and Jacobson's organ

Like all snakes (and a few lizards), rattlers use their tongues to explore and identify their surroundings. When a rattlesnake flicks its tongue out it is 'tasting' the air by picking up airborne molecules. When it withdraws its tongue into its mouth, it inserts each of its twin tips into a specialized organ embedded in the roof of its mouth, the Jacobson's organ. This is lined with nerve endings and is linked to the brain by a branch of the olfactory nerve – the same nerve that connects the nostrils to the brain. The Jacobson's organ, therefore, is an organ of smell, and the tongue conveys scents to it from the outside world. They work together to enhance the snake's sense of smell.

The pits

Rattlesnakes and their close relatives are known as pit vipers, a reference to the pits situated on either side of the face. These facial pits are sense organs, used to detect radiant heat, and are not found in other animals apart from some boas and pythons. (The pits of boas and pythons, however, are slightly different and evolved independently – an example of convergent evolution, by which unrelated animals arrive at a similar solution to a particular problem. Boas and pythons are not closely related to vipers.)

Pit vipers have a pair of pits, one on each side of the head, and located just below an imaginary line drawn from the nostril to the eye. They look rather like extra nostrils, and in parts of Central and

South America certain pit vipers (though not rattlesnakes as it happens) are called *cuatro narices*, which means 'four nostrils'. They are slightly larger than nostrils and, internally, there is a cavity in the fang-bearing bones (the maxilla) to make room for them.

The pits point forward and each has an inner and an outer chamber, separated by a diaphragm. The outer chamber is the larger of the two and its opening is the one we can see in the side of the rattlesnake's head. The pink layer that can be seen inside the pit is the surface of the diaphragm, not the bottom of the pit. The inner chamber is smaller and connects with the outside world by means of a small pore that opens in front of the eye: it is so small as to be practically invisible. There are muscles around the pore's perimeter, so that the snake can close it off. This arrangement probably allows the snake to equalize the pressure and the background temperature between the inner and outer chambers.

Heat entering the outer pit will fall on the diaphragm, which has many nerves leading to the brain. In this way, the snake can detect at a distance any object that is warmer than its general surrounding. Under normal circumstances this means other animals. The membrane is extremely sensitive and can distinguish between objects with very slight temperature differences – less than 0.2°C (0.4°F) at close range. This sensitivity has several implications.

Because of the extreme sensitivity of these pits, the rattlesnake can determine the exact position of its prey by comparing the messages received in each pit. Because the pits are quite widely spaced, it will also be able to judge its range. It is not only warm-blooded prey that can be sensed in this way; cold-blooded animals, such as lizards, that have been basking in a warm place can be detected equally well. Many young rattlers eat lizards and some of the smaller species eat them throughout their lives. So efficient are the pits that they even enable the rattlesnake to judge the best place in which to sink its fangs – rattlers 'hit' the chest region of their prey almost every time.

The venom apparatus

Rattlesnakes' fangs are similar to those of other vipers. They are long, curved, hollow structures that inject venom deep into the body of their prey. When not in use, they can be hinged out of the way and covered with a fleshy sheath so that the snake can close its

Overleaf: *A southern Pacific rattlesnake,* Crotalus viridis helleri, *using its tongue to 'taste' the air by picking up scent particles.*

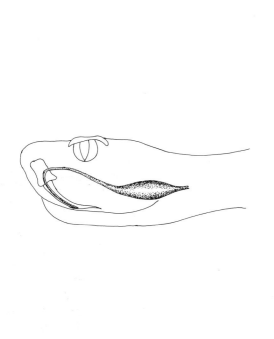
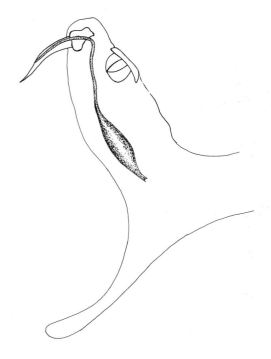

mouth. The fangs are attached to a bone called the maxilla, which is shorter than it is in other snakes and can be rotated throughout an arc of about 90°. This swings the fangs back and forward as required (Fig. 6). When the snake strikes, it normally moves both fangs into the 'armed' position, but it can move them independently of each other if necessary. It may do this when it is re-aligning its jaws after it has swallowed a meal. The fangs of vipers are different from those of other venomous snakes, such as cobras or coral snakes, which have short, fixed fangs that do not hinge.

Each fang is connected to a venom gland by a narrow tube or duct. The venom glands are located on either side of the snake's head, just behind its eyes. The snake forces venom along the duct by squeezing the venom gland with specialized muscles. The venom then enters a canal that runs up through the hollow fang and comes out through a smaller opening near its tip. Even though a bite may appear to take only a split second, the snake usually pumps the venom gland several times in order to force plenty of venom into its victim. Very occasionally the snake may make a 'dry' bite – one in which no venom is injected.

Fig. 6 *When at rest, the fangs are folded up along the roof of the snake's mouth. During the strike, they are swung down by rotating the maxillary bone, to which they are attached. The venom gland and duct are also shown.*

When at rest, the fangs are covered by fleshy sheathes. These slide back when the fangs swing into action, although they still cover their bases, gripping them tightly to prevent venom from leaking out. From time to time, fangs are replaced by new ones that grow next to the old ones, so that for a while the snake may have two pairs of fangs although the replacements for both fangs do not necessarily grow at the same time. The sheath covers both the functional fang and the replacement one while it is growing and, for a while, venom may be discharged through both of them.

The awesome fangs of an average-sized western diamondback, Crotalus atrox. *Note how the fleshy sheath covers the base of the fangs even when they are erected; this helps to prevent venom leakage.*

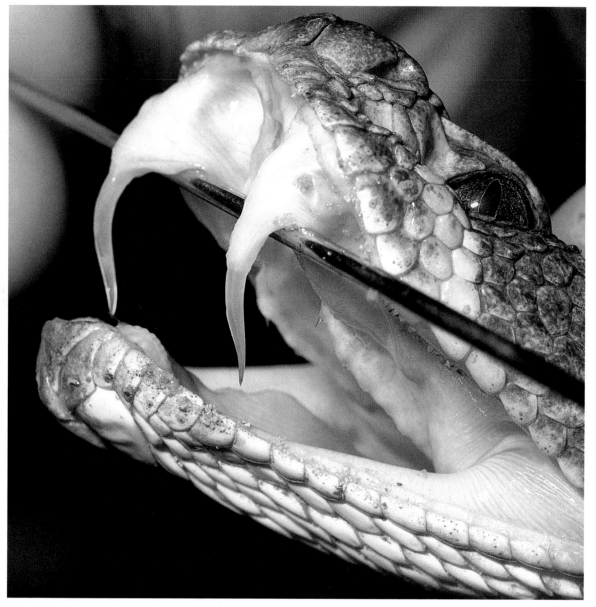

2

HABITS AND HABITATS

Rattlesnakes are interesting to look at and watch, but any study of these fascinating creatures must take account of where they live, how they came to be there and how they interact with their environment.

Distribution

Rattlesnakes of one sort or another can be found from southern Canada right down to Argentina. In some places it is possible to find only a single species whereas in other places several species may occur side by side. They are most numerous in Mexico, where 24 of the 27 species of *Crotalus*, and two of the three species of *Sistrurus* occur – indeed, 12 species of *Crotalus* and one of *Sistrurus* (*S. ravus*) do not occur anywhere else.

Two species of *Crotalus*, the eastern diamondback (*C. adamanteus*) and the timber rattlesnake (*C. horridus*), and one *Sistrurus*, the pygmy rattlesnake (*S. miliarius*), occur only in the United States. Here there are rattlesnakes in every mainland state except Alaska, Delaware and Maine. Arizona has the greatest number of species, with eleven, and there are eight species in Texas, seven in New Mexico and six in California. Two species occur in southern Canada: they are the western rattlesnake (in two forms, the northern Pacific, *Crotalus viridis oreganus*, and the prairie rattlesnake, *C. viridis viridis*), and the massassauga (*Sistrurus catenatus*).

The species with by far the widest range is the neotropical rattlesnake (*Crotalus durissus*), which extends from about 24°N in Mexico to about 35°S in central Argentina. It does not occur everywhere within these boundaries, however, because it dislikes dense rain forests and high mountain ranges. Because of this, it is not

The neotropical rattlesnake, Crotalus durissus, *is the species with the greatest distribution. This form,* C. d. culminatus, *hails from south-western Mexico. Photo by David Barker.*

found in Panama, Ecuador or Chile. Nor does it occur in the West Indies, although it is found on three islands off the Venezuelan coast – Aruba (where it is sometimes regarded as a separate species, *C. unicolor*), Margarita and Los Testigos. So vast is its range and so patchy its distribution, that there are 14 geographical races or subspecies.

At the other extreme, there are a number of species that have very restricted ranges. These include the forms found on small islands in the Gulf of California, such as *Crotalus catalinensis*, found only on Isla Santa Catalina, and *Crotalus tortugensis*, found only on Isla Tortuga. The latter appears to be closely related to the western diamondback, *C. atrox*, whereas *C. catalinensis* seems to have affinities with both the red diamond rattlesnake, *C. ruber*, and the Mojave rattlesnake, *C. scutatus*. Similarly, the Cedros Island rattlesnake, found only on Isla Cedros, off the Pacific coast of Baja California, may only be a variant of *C. ruber*. There is more about the status of these forms in Chapter 5. The rarest rattlesnake of all is *Crotalus lannomi*, of which only a single specimen has ever been collected, from Jalisco, in western Mexico. It was scientifically described in 1966 but, despite repeated attempts to locate additional specimens, nobody has managed to find one since.

Knowing the range of each species, in broad geographical terms, is not very informative, however. Most plants and animals, including rattlesnakes, are habitat specific. In other words, they are choosy about the sort of terrain in which they live. Some rattlesnakes, for instance, are confirmed lowland dwellers, while others are equally specialized mountain dwellers. The lowland species tend to have larger ranges, whereas the montane species often have small, restricted ranges. This is because mountain ranges tend to be isolated from one another by expanses of different types of habitat, such as grasslands, deserts and so on, preventing the migration and spread of snakes from one mountain range to the next. For this reason, isolated mountain ranges are often called 'ecological islands'.

Populations of rattlesnakes that are cut off from neighbouring ones like this can evolve in different ways, and the longer they are isolated the greater is the likelihood that different species will arise. Lowland species have no such barriers – their populations may be absent from the mountain ranges but there is plenty of opportunity for them to spread between and around the mountains, intermingling with one another and allowing genes to flow freely from one part of the population to another.

The pattern that emerges from this is a mosaic, consisting of relatively few lowland species, like the western diamondback, the

Mojave rattler and the western rattlesnake, which are spread across wide areas and, within these areas, scattered populations of montane rattlesnakes, each of which has a relatively small range.

Habitats

Dry rocky places in the deserts of south-western United States and north-western Mexico are the habitats of several specialized rattlers such as the tiger and speckled rattlesnakes as well as a number of more generalized species, such as the Mojave and western diamondback rattlers.

Looking at habitats in more detail, we see that rattlesnakes occupy a number of distinct types of habitat, but avoid several others that are available to them. For example, there are no aquatic, arboreal or burrowing rattlesnakes. Although it is possible to find the odd one in water, up a tree or in a shrub, these are exceptions – perhaps snakes that have found themselves in an unusual situation by accident. Similarly, although rattlesnakes do not burrow in the true sense of the word, the sidewinder does shuffle down into the sand. Other species also spend a great deal of their time below the surface but in natural crevices or in burrows that they have taken over from other animals such as rodents.

One possible explanation of why rattlesnakes avoid certain habitats is that they evolved in dry, terrestrial environments and have become too specialized to try out others. In particular, their rattle, which is an asset to them in their preferred habitats, could become a distinct liability if they tried to swim, climb or burrow. Similarly, their facial pits would not function well under water or below ground. So, rattlesnakes have a limited number of options.

Moist places are not very attractive to rattlesnakes. Only the massasauga (*Sistrurus catenatus*) is at all associated with this kind of habitat and then only the populations towards the north-east of its range. Here it occurs in damp prairies, meadows and bogs for part of the year, although it migrates to higher and drier woods and fields for the summer. Rattlesnakes from the south-eastern United States, such as the eastern diamondback (*Crotalus adamanteus*) and the pygmy rattler (*Sistrurus miliarius*), may live in damp regions but usually keep to quite dry microhabitats at the edges of swamps and savannahs.

Many species live in deserts and arid, scrub-covered, semi-desert regions. These include the sidewinder (*Crotalus cerastes*), which occurs only where there is loose sand and sparse vegetation, and a number of more generalized species, such as the western diamondback (*C. atrox*), Mojave (*C. scutulatus*) and western (*C. viridis*) rattlesnakes, that thrive in all sorts of desert habitats. Rocky areas within deserts are the home of a good number of species, including the three generalists listed above, as well as the red diamond (*C. ruber*), speckled (*C. mitchellii*) and tiger (*C. tigris*) rattlesnakes. Montane species are very numerous, especially in Mexico, although a few species also spill over the border into the southern United States. They include the rock (*C. lepidus*), twin-spot (*C. pricei*) and ridge-nosed (*C. willardi*) rattlesnakes. All these live in high, rocky places, especially south-facing, boulder-strewn slopes and talus slides. Other highland species favour grassy meadows and clearings in forests of pine and oak. These include Mexican species such as *C. pusillus*, *C. polystictus*, *C. triseriatus* and *C. transversus*, also some of the species that are restricted to south-facing slopes further north, such as *C. willardi* and *C. pricei*.

So, in order to find or understand rattlesnakes it is not enough to know in which part of the world each type lives. You also need to know whether it prefers mountains, deserts or prairies. Even this is not the end of the story. Rattlesnakes have very specialized needs, and within each large habitat there will be a number of smaller ones; habitats within habitats. These microhabitats are the sorts of places

Slopes of loose weathered rock, known as talus slides in America and scree slopes in Europe, are the home of specialized montane species such as the twin-spotted rattlesnake, Crotalus pricei, *and the rock rattlesnake,* Crotalus lepidus.

that rattlesnakes prefer to spend their time – a south-facing, boulder-strewn slope; along a river course; on loose, windblown sand dunes, etc. Because there are many microhabitats within a given area and because some species limit themselves to one type of microhabitat, it is sometimes possible for several species to live in close proximity to one another without ever competing. Biologists call this habitat sharing or niche separation.

ALTITUDE

The Mexican dusky rattlesnake (*Crotalus triseriatus*) lives at elevations of up to 4,572m (15,000ft) in central Mexico, which is higher than any other American snake. (As a matter of interest, the highest occurring snake in the Old World is also a pit viper and therefore closely related to rattlesnakes. It is *Agkistrodon himalayanus*, a snake which lives at an altitude of up to 4,877m (16,000ft) in the Himalayas.) As one travels north, the higher mountains become untenable for rattlesnakes because of the severity of the climate there, especially in winter. In the United States, therefore, the highest altitude attained by a rattlesnake is probably somewhere between 3,300 and 3,500 metres (10,800–11,500ft), by the western rattlesnake (*C. viridis*) in the Sierra Nevada mountain range of southern California. This rattlesnake has an especially wide elevation range, because it also occurs below sea-level around the Salton Sea, along with the sidewinder. The sidewinder also occurs below sea-level in Death Valley, but the western rattlesnake is absent from there.

Behaviour

LOCOMOTION

Rattlesnakes use three distinct methods of getting from one place to another: serpentine crawling, rectilinear crawling and sidewinding. The first two are common to all terrestrial snakes, but sidewinding is peculiar to one rattlesnake and a few African vipers that live in similar habitats.

Serpentine crawling

In this method of locomotion the snake uses its flanks to push against small irregularities on the surface. Each part of the snake pushes against the same points of contact in sequence so that the tracks, if visible, would consist of a parallel-sided 'wiggle'. This is the 'standard' method of locomotion for rattlesnakes.

Rectilinear locomotion

In straight-line crawling, the snake behaves more like a caterpillar, but using its ventral scales where the insect would use its feet. The snake pushes each ventral scale forward in turn and hooks its trailing edge over irregularities. This gives it enough grip to pull up the next set of ventral scales and hook their edges, in turn, over the same irregularities. This process is going on along the whole length of the snake so that, at any given time, some sections are pulling while the sections between are being pulled. The effect is a smooth, gliding motion, and the tracks form a straight furrow. Large, heavy-bodied rattlesnakes use this type of locomotion, especially when they are moving across ground that has no large objects against which they can push. In addition, all rattlesnakes tend to use this locomotion if they are moving up quietly on their prey to get within striking distance.

Sidewinders, Crotalus cerastes, *occur only where there is a sandy substrate and little or no vegetation. They move across loose sand in a series of looping movements, producing distinctive tracks.*

Sidewinding

Sidewinding is performed, not surprisingly, by the sidewinder! It starts by raising its head off the ground and throwing it sideways. By the time the head has landed, several inches further along, a loop of the body will have followed it. Before the tail has taken up its new position, however, the snake will have thrown its head sideways again to begin the next cycle. The overall effect is of a snake rapidly skimming over the surface and making progress at an angle of about 45° to the line of its body. Because every part of its body leaves the surface at some stage, its tracks consist of a series of unconnected J-shaped marks in the sand.

ACTIVITY PATTERNS

Like all reptiles, rattlesnakes cannot produce their own body heat as we can. They have to rely on outside sources of warmth and this, directly or indirectly, means the sun. They may gain heat by basking in the sun's rays or by pressing their body against objects, such as rocks, that have been warmed by the sun. There are some regions where the temperature of the air itself is sufficiently high to maintain the snake's body temperature. A burst of sun basking in the morning may be all that is necessary to reach, and then keep, a correct operating temperature through the day. On the other hand, although they need to be warm, they can also die from overheating, and in very hot places they may need to shelter from the heat for part of the day.

Temperature, then, dictates their activity patterns to a very large extent and other factors, such as food supply, are less important. Although the species may differ by a few degrees in their preferred temperatures, they all need to be at around 30°C (86°F) to operate efficiently. At temperatures much lower than this they have trouble in digesting food and moving around. If the temperature reaches much higher than this they can die of heat exhaustion. Understanding the way in which they regulate their temperature is the key to understanding their activity patterns.

Daily and seasonal activity patterns

Two factors have a bearing on the temperature of any environment: place and time. Generally speaking, places that are at high latitudes are usually colder than those that are near the equator, and mountains are usually colder than lowlands. In addition, there are seasonal and daily temperature cycles. Rattlesnakes' lives are closely linked to these cycles, and their activity patterns often change throughout the year to reflect these differences. We can illustrate this principle by looking at the activity patterns of rattlesnakes that live in different places.

A recent study by Richard Seigel[1] concerns the activity pattern of a population of massassaugas (*Sistrurus catenatus*) living in Missouri. Dr Seigel found that the massassaugas in his study site (a wildlife refuge) were active from mid-April until late October, 193 days per year on average. During the spring and the autumn he found that most of them were active between midday and 4 p.m., and smaller

1. Richard A. Seigel, 1986, 'Ecology and conservation of an endangered rattlesnake, *Sistrurus catenatus*, in Missouri, U.S.A.', *Biological Conservation*, 35: 333–346.

numbers were active in the morning, late afternoon and evening. In the summer, however, most of the activity took place between 4 p.m. and 8 p.m. In the summer (and to a lesser extent in the spring) massassaugas were also active during the night, whereas in the autumn they were not. During the winter, massassaugas were not active at all.

Some of the central Mexican rattlesnakes that occur at high altitudes have a rather similar pattern, although they have not been as thoroughly studied. In the places where they live, the nights are too cold for them to be active, even in the summer, so they are totally diurnal. They emerge from their night-time retreats as soon as the ground has warmed up – on sunny, summer days this may be early in the mornings but during spring and autumn only the middle part of the day is suitable for them.

By comparison, rattlesnakes living in low, desert regions have less problem keeping warm but must be careful to avoid extreme heat. Western diamondbacks, for instance, are first seen in early spring, when they begin to emerge to bask and feed in the afternoon. As the weather warms up, they are abroad later and later until, by summer, they do not come above the surface at all during daylight hours: they become totally nocturnal. Even throughout the night, though, there can be differences in their activity times. In spring and early summer the desert nights can be quite cold and as soon as the surface cools down, some time before midnight, the snakes go underground. At the height of summer they may be active until well after midnight.

Although these rules of thumb are good enough to describe rattlesnake activity patterns in general terms, there are one or two complications. Firstly, some species have strict nocturnal habits and seem to be reluctant to emerge during daylight hours even if this is best for them in terms of temperature. The tiger rattlesnake is one of these species. Secondly, rattlesnake activity is greater in the spring than one would expect from temperature alone. This is because male rattlesnakes spend much of their time in the spring and early summer looking for potential mates. This often involves travelling, even though the temperature may not be as warm as they would like. The urge to reproduce overcomes the urge to keep warm.

Rattlesnakes' activity patterns, of course, have a bearing on our perception of them. In the summer, in the desert, we will see rattlesnakes only if we are out after dark and many are seen (and killed) on desert roads at night. If we look in the mountains at the same time of the year, though, we will see them only if we look during the warmer parts of the day. This can also apply *within* a species if it occurs in both the lowlands and in mountains; in the summer, the lowland populations will be nocturnal whereas the montane populations will be diurnal. Each snake will adjust its activity pattern to the prevailing conditions, irrespective of what its relatives may be doing elsewhere.

Hibernation

During the winter, temperatures do not rise high enough in most places for rattlesnakes to be active at all. The exceptions are lowland Central and South America where a few species, notably the neotropical rattlesnake (*Crotalus durissus*) live. All other species have to find a way of surviving the cold winter period and they do this by hibernating.

Hibernation can take several forms. In warmer areas it may only be necessary for the snakes to take shelter for a limited period, perhaps a few days or weeks at a time, interspersed with warmer periods when they can emerge and become active again. These species shelter singly or in small groups numbering a few individuals, perhaps coming together by chance because they each find the same crevice or burrow. In colder places, however, such as northern latitudes and in the mountains, a more or less continuous period of hibernation is necessary, sometimes for many months. Timber rattlesnakes at the northern edge of their range, for instance, hibernate for more than seven months each year. Where the density of snakes is high and suitable sites are rare, rattlesnakes congregate in large dens in deep crevices in rocks or in holes and galleries in the earth such as those made by prairie dogs. Rocky dens are often south-facing.

Several hundred rattlesnakes may use the same den. Some of the largest dens have unfortunately been destroyed, and the huge numbers recorded in the past will probably never be seen again. The northerly occurring forms of the western rattlesnake, such as the prairie rattlesnake (*Crotalus viridis viridis*), the Great Basin rattlesnake (*C. v. lutosus*) and the northern Pacific rattlesnake (*C. v. oreganus*), are thought to form the largest aggregations, exceptionally up to 1,000 individuals. Other western species that group together to hibernate include the western diamondback, the red diamond rattlesnake and the speckled rattlesnake. These species are found in smaller numbers, however, usually under 50 to a den.

In the east the only species that forms reasonably large dens seems to be the timber rattler (*C. horridus horridus*), with over 200 having been recorded at several locations earlier this century. Numbers of this species have now been severely depleted, however. Eastern diamondbacks (*C. adamanteus*) are sometimes found together, especially under large tree stumps or in holes where large trees have fallen, but only in moderate numbers. The habits of the species from central Mexico have not been studied in detail.

Rattlesnakes that hibernate in den sites often spend several days in the spring basking near the entrance before they disperse. This is known as 'lying out'. A second lying out period takes place in the autumn before they go down into the den, but this tends to be shorter. Traditionally, rattlesnake hunts or 'roundups' used to take place during the lying out period so that the maximum number of snakes could be slaughtered.

HOME RANGES

Most rattlesnakes appear to have home ranges – areas within which they can predictably be found. Their normal home ranges may be well away from the places where they hibernate, however, so some snakes may travel quite long distances each spring and autumn when they are migrating to and from their dens. Having a home range probably helps the snakes to feed more efficiently because they get to know their 'patch' and can predict the places where food is likely to be. This pattern holds true for most of the species that have been studied. Sidewinders, however, appear to be different. It would seem that each night they wander in a random fashion over a very large tract of desert. At the end of their period of activity they shuffle down into the sand to hide. The following day they remain just below the surface, perhaps hoping to ambush prey, or, if the temperature becomes dangerously high, they find a rodent burrow in which to shelter.

FEEDING

After temperature regulation, feeding is one of the most important rattlesnake activities. Their feeding habits have, to a large extent, been the driving force behind the evolution of their venom apparatus and, ultimately, the rattle.

Types of prey

Considering the number of species and the wide range of different habitats in which they live, rattlesnakes have a fairly predictable menu. Since their most specialized sense organs, the heat pits, evolved to detect the presence of warm objects, it is hardly surprising that warm-blooded prey figure most highly.

Their most important food, by far, is mammals. There are probably no species of rattlesnake that do not eat mammals, at least occasionally, and many species eat nothing else. Taking an overall average, rattlesnakes' diets consist of about 85 per cent mammals. The type of mammal varies somewhat according to the size of the rattlesnake and, of course, its location. It is unlikely that rattlers have any particular preference among species but merely eat whatever is available, provided it can fit into their mouths. Their commonest prey species will usually be the species that is commonest where they live. These include mice of several genera, kangaroo and wood rats and slightly larger mammals, such as chipmunks, ground squirrels, prairie dogs, squirrels and cottontail rabbits. The young of some of these larger species are as much as some rattlesnakes can manage, and they probably take them by raiding nests, but the larger rattlers can accommodate adults of all the species listed. Rattlesnakes can take relatively large prey and sometimes eat items that are almost their own weight. Other vipers are equally capacious, but snakes in other families are restricted to prey that is relatively much smaller.

From a number of studies carried out on the diet of rattlesnakes, one can see their effectiveness in controlling populations of rodents and lagomorphs (rabbits and hares). In one part of Idaho, for instance, prairie rattlesnakes eat 14 per cent of the local ground squirrel population and up to 11 per cent of the cottontail rabbit population every year. The part that they play in the local ecological balance is therefore very significant (as is their benefit to local agriculture).

Birds form the second most important class of prey, about 10 per cent on average. Predictably, most of the birds concerned are ground-nesting ones such as quail, but rattlesnakes also climb into low bushes and shrubs in search of nestlings and roosting adults. Domestic birds are probably taken occasionally, but compared with other predators rattlesnakes are relatively unimportant to poultry farmers. The massasauga sometimes eats birds' eggs.

The remaining 5 per cent of the rattlesnakes' diet consists of amphibians, lizards and other snakes. The smaller species and the young of some of the larger ones may live primarily on lizards. Lizards, however, are 'cold-blooded' and, although their body

A Queretaran dusky rattlesnake, Crotalus aquilus, *swallows a mouse. Rattlesnakes can engulf large prey by stretching their jaws and skin, and using their fangs to pull the item into their throats. A single meal like this may be the result of staking out a likely spot for several days. Photo by David Barker.*

temperatures may be higher than those of their surroundings if they have been basking, the rattlesnakes' heat pits have probably not evolved primarily to take advantage of this type of prey. It may be that lizards became the prey of rattlesnakes whose size became reduced after the pits had already appeared.

Amphibians are also cold-blooded and should therefore be regarded as an 'abnormal' type of prey for rattlesnakes, but the species that live in damp places probably eat them occasionally. We might expect species such as the massassauga to feed on frogs and toads because it is commonly associated with swamps and damp meadows. This would be quite wrong, however, because, as Richard Seigel has pointed out, adults of this species seems to feed almost exclusively on voles and mice while the juveniles also eat small snakes (see footnote on page 42).

Method of hunting

Finding and subduing prey takes up a large proportion of every rattlesnake's waking hours, not because they eat large numbers of prey but because finding and catching them is time-consuming. Rattlesnakes are 'sit-and-wait' predators, by which we mean that they wait in a suitable place, hoping to ambush a tasty morsel. It is probable that many nights are unproductive and so the rattlesnake's success as a hunter relies largely on its patience.

If we take a typical, hypothetical rattlesnake and follow its routine, we may find that it goes something as follows, allowing for variations on its locality and the time of year. Activity begins when the sun sets and the ground begins to cool. This is also the time when rodents become most active above ground. Having roused itself, our rattler makes for a likely place in which to lie in wait for its quarry, perhaps somewhere that smells strongly of rodents or perhaps a place where it has been successful in the past. The journey may be quite a long one and may involve negotiating several hazards, such as open places where predators may be watching or, worse still, roads.

Having safely reached its chosen spot, the rattler coils up against a rock or among low vegetation and waits. It puts a couple of shallow bends into its neck so that it is ready to strike as soon as a potential meal comes within range and rests its head on its coils. Time passes and nothing stirs. Gradually the ground loses the heat it absorbed during the day. After a few hours, the rattler's body temperature approaches the critical level where locomotion will become difficult, making it vulnerable to attack. Hunting must be abandoned for the night and our snake returns to its retreat, its appetite unsatisfied.

Ground squirrels form an important part of the diet of rattlesnakes that live where they occur.

This, or a similar chain of events, may be repeated for several more nights – it seems that rattlesnakes and related species often wait several days or even weeks before prey materializes. After a series of unsuccessful nights, the snake may wait in a different place – evolution will have told it how long to persevere in one place and when to try another (human hunters, fishermen and fruit-pickers all have to make similar decisions, although their lives rarely depend on them).

When prey finally does appear, the rattler's formidable array of sense organs comes into play. It may be alerted at first by the vibrations caused by the scurrying activities of its quarry. It begins to flicker its tongue, picking up scent molecules from the air and transferring them to the specialized Jacobson's organ in the roof of its mouth. This supplements the snake's sense of smell and is extremely sensitive. Having identified the source of the vibrations – a pocket mouse, perhaps – it uses its heat pits to pinpoint its whereabouts. Even if the mouse senses danger and 'freezes' it will continue to radiate heat from its body. Balancing the messages it receives in each pit, the snake accurately judges the mouse's range as well as its position. If the mouse is beyond its striking range, and seems unlikely to come any closer, the snake edges forward slightly, using its ventral scales to pull itself over the ground in a continuous flowing movement.

It may stalk the mouse like this for some time, until it is within range. It pauses momentarily, then strikes. During the strike it opens its mouth wide and swings its fangs forward so that they point directly at the mouse. As they make contact the snake clamps its jaws shut and pumps venom through its fangs by compressing the muscles surrounding its venom glands. Then it releases the mouse and returns to its coiled position. Only a second or so has passed. It may open and close its mouth a few times to re-align the jaw bones and fold away the fangs. Meanwhile, the mouse begins to stagger and gasp for breath. It crawls around helplessly, becoming progressively weaker.

After a few minutes, the snake begins to flick its tongue over the ground where the mouse was struck. Its picks up its scent and tracks it until it finds the body. Now it searches for the head and begins to swallow, using first one fang then the other to pull the carcass into its mouth until it has engulfed it, finally using muscular contractions of its throat to send it on its way to the stomach. By now, an hour or more may have passed since the snake first detected the mouse. The digestive process will already be well under way, thanks to the enzymes in the venom. The snake's patience has paid off.

A rat's eye view of a San Lucas rattlesnake. Note how the pits point forward, scanning the area immediately in front of the snake. This is the form of red diamondback rattlesnake that inhabits the Cape region of Baja California, currently known as Crotalus ruber lucasensis.

Now it may reposition itself and wait for another meal but it is more likely to make its way back to its retreat and, if the meal was a large one, it will remain there for a few days to digest it.

Our rattler may not always follow these classic ambush tactics. Sometimes it might poke about in likely places in the hope of finding an easier meal such as a litter of nestling rodents, or its keen olfactory senses may lead it to prey that is already dead, such as a road kill. Rattlesnakes are thought to be more likely to take advantage of carrion than many other kinds of snakes because they are already 'programmed' to take dead prey – that is, prey that they have killed themselves. They have, on occasion, been seen devouring animals that have been dead for several hours or even days.

VENOM: ITS COMPOSITION AND EFFECTS

Snake venom is one of the most complex, naturally occurring organic substances. It performs two important functions for the snake: overcoming its prey and deterring its enemies. The first of these is the more important and is widely believed to be the reason it evolved in the first place. Venom is used in defence only as a last resort – camouflage, escape, intimidation (by rattling, hissing and mock strikes) are usually the first lines of defence. Venom also plays a part in the digestion of the snake's prey, in some cases initiating the process before it is even swallowed. This is by no means an essential function, however, and rattlesnakes will eat and digest prey that has not been envenomated, including carrion, although in such cases digestion may take longer.

Rattlesnake venom consists largely of proteins, mainly in the form of enzymes. There are at least 10 different enzymes in all snake venoms and that of some species can contain over 20. Enzymes cause biochemical reactions inside or outside animal cells, effectively breaking them down. In effect, snake venom is a very strong solution of digestive juices that can be injected into another animal by biting. Because the composition of the venom differs from species to species, its effects also differ. There is some evidence to suggest that venoms of different types have evolved to be most effective on the prey species most often eaten by the species in question.

The strength of a snake's venom depends on several factors. While the venom of some species is more potent than that of others, the amount that the snake injects, known as the 'yield', is also important. Usually, large species have a higher yield than small ones. The type of venom is also an important factor. Although snake venoms are extremely variable, they can be crudely grouped into 'families'. Venomous snakes produce cocktails of venom containing more than one variety, although one type of venom usually predominates. Snake bite symptoms vary according to which part of the venom is most effective.

Most viper venoms act mainly on the blood and the circulatory system of their prey. Venoms of this type are known as 'haemotoxic'. The other important type of venom acts on the nervous system of the prey, and this is known as 'neurotoxic' venom. Although it can be dangerous to generalize, neurotoxins tend to act more quickly than haemotoxins. They also produce little pain or tissue damage at the site of the bite but cause breathing difficulties and paralysis. Haemotoxins cause immediate pain at the site of the bite, massive bruising and internal haemorrhaging, followed by permanent tissue damage.

Our knowledge of rattlesnake venoms is incomplete. Only the most common species and, more specifically, the common species that occur in the United States have attracted very much attention. The venoms of many Mexican rattlesnakes, especially the small montane species, are hardly known at all.

One of the commonest rattlesnakes is the western diamondback (*Crotalus atrox*) and this will serve as a typical or 'base line' species with which to compare some of the others. Yields of venom from this species (measured by milking the snakes) average about 400mg but vary from 175 to over 1,000mg (dry weight). This seemingly wild variation is due to differences in the size of the snake, how long since it last bit something and how well it was milked. The eastern diamondback (*C. adamanteus*) has a similar yield, but these two are way ahead of the next highest yields, which come from the red diamond rattlesnake (*C. ruber*), the timber rattler (*C. horridus horridus*) and the black-tailed rattler (*C. molossus*). Medium-sized rattlesnakes, such as the various forms of the prairie rattlesnake (*Crotalus viridis*), yield up to about 400mg, but again there is great variation. Small species, such as the sidewinder, the massassauga and pygmy rattlesnake, rarely produce more than 50mg or about one-eighth of the average yield of a western diamondback.

Potency of rattlesnake venom is measured in 'lethal doses'. The method of establishing this is to inject batches of standard laboratory mice, each weighing 20g, with venom. The amount of venom is varied by dilution until the dose kills 50 per cent of the mice. This is called the 50 per cent lethal dose or LD_{50}. The smaller the figure, the more potent the venom. LD_{50} is usually expressed in terms of mg

per kg, which is the amount required to kill 50 mice each weighing 20 grams. A convenient measure of the danger of a rattlesnake's bite is to combine the LD_{50} and the yield. This figure gives us the number of lethal doses a snake could give to 20g mice if it used up all the venom in its glands.

The LD_{50} of western diamondback venom is about 5mg per kg. This is quite mild compared with most other rattlesnakes, but because the yield is so high it is still a very dangerous species – a western diamondback contains enough venom, on average, to kill 4,000 mice. The LD_{50} of the black-tailed rattlesnake is about the same as that of the western diamondback, but it has a lower yield, producing enough venom to kill almost 3,000 mice, on average. The eastern diamondback's venom, however, is about twice as potent as that of the western diamondback, and, because its yield is roughly the same, its produces about 8,000 'lethal mouse doses'.

All of the species we have looked at so far produce mainly haemotoxic venom. This type tends not to be as potent as neurotoxic venom and so larger quantities are required to kill prey of similar size. A few rattlesnakes, however, produce mainly neurotoxic venom. The most infamous of these is the Mojave rattlesnake (*C. scutulatus*), of which there are two forms: a haemotoxin-producing one and a neurotoxin-producing one. The first type has an LD_{50} of about 3mg per kg and a yield of about 70mg, so it is capable of producing enough venom to kill just over 1,000 mice – it is about one-quarter as dangerous as the western diamondback. The second type, however, has much more powerful venom, with an LD_{50} of about 0.24mg per kg. It has the same 70mg yield as the other type and so its killing capacity is in the region of 15,000 mice – nearly four times that of the western diamondback and making it far and away the most dangerous North American rattlesnake.

Certain forms of the neotropical rattlesnake are slightly more dangerous, though, especially the subspecies *C. durissus terrificus*. The LD_{50} of this rattler is about the same as the Mojave rattlesnake but it has a higher yield, up to 100mg.

Other rattlesnakes that produce neurotoxins include the tiger rattlesnake (*C. tigris*) and certain populations of the speckled rattlesnake (*C. mitchellii*) with an LD_{50} of 0.3, an average yield of 30–40mg of venom and about 5,000 lethal mouse doses, and some populations of the rock rattlesnake (*C. lepidus*) with an LD_{50} of 0.5.

In places, the Mojave rattlesnake, Crotalus scutulatus, *is the most dangerous North American species because it produces a particularly potent cocktail of venoms.*

This species has a low yield, however, about 10mg, which is enough venom to kill about 1,000 mice.

Why should a few species or populations of rattlesnakes produce a far more potent venom than all the others? Neurotoxins usually act faster than haemotoxic ones and their evolution could be due to differences in habitat, a shift in prey type or both. Imagine a rattlesnake that lives in a rocky place. This individual would need to kill its prey quickly, otherwise it might crawl off and die in an inaccessible crevice. This would be especially important if the prey was a lizard, which is slender and able to enter smaller places than a mammal. In addition, venoms do not act as quickly on lizards because they have lower metabolic rates than mammals. A lizard that has time to jam itself into a tight space before it succumbs to the venom is a lost meal.

Nobody knows if this is the answer to this particular puzzle, but there is some circumstantial evidence. At least some of the rattlesnakes with fast-acting neurotoxic venom live in rocky places and three of them, the rock, speckled and tiger rattlesnakes, have small, narrow heads, which may have evolved for retrieving food from narrow crevices.

Regardless of its composition, venom can be effective only if there is a suitable means of delivering it to the places where it can be most effective. Rattlers' long, curved fangs are well suited to this task. In particular, the ability to fold them away when not in use is important: it means they can be longer than would be possible if they were fixed. Long fangs allow the snake to bite deep into the body of its prey and inject the venom straight into its trunk, where it can take effect very quickly, killing it before it has time to travel very far. Experiments have shown that when a prairie rattlesnake bites it injects 89 per cent of the venom into the prey's body and leaves only 11 per cent on its skin.[2]

DEFENCE

Rattlesnakes have a number of enemies, against which they are well-equipped to defend themselves. Large mammals may trample them, either intentionally or accidentally, and it is likely that the rattle evolved to avoid just this possibility. Carnivorous mammals, such as foxes, coyotes and badgers, eat rattlesnakes, as do domestic animals

2 W. K. Hayes, I. I. Kaiser and D. Duvall, 1992, 'The mass of venom expended by prairie rattlesnakes when feeding on rodent prey', in *Biology of the Pit Vipers* (edited by J. A. Campbell and E. D. Brodie), Selva, Texas: 383–388.

The heads of the rock rattlesnake, Crotalus lepidus, *and a couple of other species, are characteristically small, perhaps so that they can retrieve prey from narrow crevices.*

such as dogs and cats, although none of these animals specialize in eating snakes. Some birds of prey, especially the red-tailed hawk, eat a substantial number of rattlesnakes. Other birds may eat them occasionally, although the roadrunner's rattlesnake-killing exploits are probably exaggerated.

Other snakes frequently eat rattlesnakes. The most important of these is the common kingsnake (*Lampropeltis getula*), but there are other species that eat them as well. These species seems to be immune to rattlesnake venom and, although they do not go out of their way to select them, they probably account for a substantial number in regions where they are common. Kingsnakes coil around their prey, usually killing it by asphyxiation and restricting its blood circulation before swallowing it. Rattlesnakes are apparently eaten before they are dead, probably because constricting would take too long. A kingsnake will grasp a rattlesnake behind its head, throw four or five coils around its body and begin to swallow almost immediately, pulling it through its coils as it does so. Rattlesnakes may be able to distinguish kingsnakes and other predatory species, because they sometimes take on particular defensive postures when they are present, holding a loop of their body off the ground, presumably to make themselves look bigger than they really are.

In addition to their response to kingsnakes, which is unique, rattlesnakes have a number of other responses. The most important of these is camouflage. By keeping still, the rattlesnake tries to blend into its surroundings, which it often matches with remarkable accuracy, both in colour and in texture. As we have already seen, there is no way of knowing how effective this strategy is – we only know when it doesn't work! If the snake feels it will be discovered despite its camouflage, perhaps because it has been caught in the open, it will usually try to crawl away quickly and find a suitable retreat. In deserts, rattlesnakes often crawl into bushes, many of which are prickly, whereas montane species crawl among rocks.

If all attempts to avoid confrontation fail, the rattlesnake moves to active defence, by trying to intimidate its enemy. It is at this point that they use their rattles.

It is worth emphasizing that rattlesnakes use their rattles only in defence. Earlier speculation that they used them to communicate with each other or to charm their prey are wrong for a very fundamental reason: rattlesnakes only rattle, or 'sound off', when they are threatened. At other times, the rattle is silent. When they move they hold the rattle parallel to the ground and just above it; the shape of the segments is designed in such a way that the rattle does not droop. This is just as well, since rattlers often employ stealth to get within striking distance of their quarry, and this would be impossible if they allowed the rattle to clatter about as they crept forward.

The rattle has a dual function. It helps to prevent the snake from being trampled to death by large grazing animals such as bison (bearing in mind that bison were once exceedingly numerous). It also warns potential predators that the snake is venomous. The only problem with the latter theory is that it requires a previous encounter between the predator and a rattlesnake, which the predator is unlikely to have survived. Even so, the noise of a rattler sounding off close by can be both startling and intimidating – certainly enough to make a predator think twice before attacking.

When a rattler wants to sound off it raises its tail to a roughly vertical position and vibrates its tip so that the segments rattle against one another, producing the characteristic sound. In fact, 'rattle' is not a very good description of the sound, which is more of a rasping buzz or even a hiss. (The Spanish name 'cascabel' is equally inaccurate because it means 'little bell' and nothing could be less like the tinkling of a little bell than a rattlesnake sounding off!) At a distance, rattlers can sound like cicadas, crickets or grasshoppers, although they usually sustain the sound for longer.

Although there is some variation in the quality of sound between the species, the main difference is in its volume. Small rattlesnakes make smaller sounds, and the pygmy rattlers, which have minute rattles, produce a low buzz that can hardly be heard. The intensity of sound also varies according to the extent of the snake's excitement – a mildly aroused snake may produce a ticking sound, but once it becomes really angry it vibrates its rattle harder and the sound builds up to a crescendo. They do this by increasing the amount of 'travel' of the rattle and also the frequency. Temperature also has a bearing on the frequency, the number of cycles or 'shakes' per second being higher when the temperature is raised. Laurence Klauber (see Further Reading, page 140) measured the frequency in a number of species at varying temperatures and found that they were fairly constant at 40 to 60 cycles per second. The highest speed he recorded was 66.9 cycles per second, which occurred in a prairie rattlesnake at 23°C (73°F) and the lowest frequency was 28.1 cycles per second, in the same species but at 11°C (52°F). This fits in well with what we already know about snakes' levels of activity being dependent on temperature.

Rattling is often accompanied by other defensive behaviour patterns, some of which are more subtle than rattling and others that are anything but subtle. Many rattlesnakes have a special defensive coil that they assume when they are threatened. They raise their heads well off the ground and make a loop with their necks. The rest of their coils are drawn up neatly to provide a good anchor point should they feel the need to strike and the rattle is raised, usually in the centre of the coils. They do not use this posture when they are hunting food. When taking up this posture they may also rattle but often they do not, depending partly on species.

Although it has been stated that rattlesnakes do not hiss like other snakes, this is incorrect. The sound of the rattle may mask other sounds that they produce, but most species will also hiss when placed under extreme provocation.

A western diamondback, Crotalus atrox, 'sounding off'. At the same time as it lifts and vibrates its rattle, it raises its head and bends its neck back so that it is ready to strike if an enemy comes within range. This particularly belligerent specimen was photographed on the small island of San Pedro Martir, in the Gulf of California. Note how its rattle is blurred, despite a fast shutter speed.

They also make a great display of the tongue, which they protrude for an extended period. Sometimes they point it downwards but at other times they curl it up and over their snout. They often spread the twin tips widely when they do this. There is no way of knowing the function of this particular aspect of behaviour – they are not trying to identify scent particles in the air because they need to return the tongue into the mouth and place its tips into the Jacobson's organ in order to do this.

Finally, rattlesnakes are, as everybody knows, quite prepared to strike and bite if all else fails. Sometimes they make ineffective lunges or 'mock' strikes first, perhaps with their mouths closed. When they do bite, they may withold venom, resulting in a 'dry' bite. A rattler's strike is rapid – about 2–3m (6–10ft) per second – and can reach a distance of about half its body length. The strike is sometimes so violent that its whole body slides forward and, under exceptional circumstance, it may completely leave the ground.

RATTLESNAKE IMITATORS

Like all good performers, rattlesnakes have their share of imitators. Foremost among them, predictably enough, are other snakes, several of which look superficially like rattlers – minus the rattle, of course. Several species of harmless colubrid snakes, notably the fox snake, some ratsnakes, gopher snakes and hognose snakes are similar in colour and markings to rattlers. Several of them also have the habit of vibrating the tips of their tails when they are alarmed and, if they happen to be resting among dry leaves or other forms of dead vegetation, this can produce a sound that bears a passable resemblance to a rattler sounding off. It is doubtful if these snakes are actively mimicking rattlesnakes, however, because tail vibrating is fairly widespread and extends to species that are found well outside the rattlesnake's range.

Other harmless species put on a show of aggression that may also lead predators to believe they are dealing with rattlesnakes. The hognose snakes, for instance, rear their heads, puff up their bodies and hiss loudly. If this is ineffective, they make lunging strikes, usually with their mouths closed, and they are frequently mistaken for rattlesnakes or other venomous species. Bull snakes raise their

Overleaf: A Mexican black-tailed rattlesnake, Crotalus molossus nigrescens, displaying its tongue in response to a threat. The significance of this piece of behaviour, which can often be seen in various rattlesnake species, is not known. Photo by David Barker.

heads and necks off the ground, open their mouths and produce a terrific hiss. Even though it is harmless, many predators are reluctant to take on an angry bull snake.

Most remarkable of all, though, is the behaviour of nestling burrowing owls (*Athene cunicularia*), which give off a sound that closely imitates that of a rattler if they are disturbed in their burrow. Few mammalian predators would care to tackle a rattler underground, and the owls' behaviour is undoubtedly effective, at least some of the time.

The western hognose snake, Heterodon nasicus, *is a famous bluffer and looks sufficiently like a rattlesnake in colour and markings to fool some predators.*

TEMPERAMENT

The temperament of rattlesnakes is at least partly related to their defensive behaviour. People who have wide experience of rattlers usually agree that some species are more bad-tempered than others. Where there are discrepancies between one person's experience and another's they are perhaps more likely to be connected to the circumstances under which each individual snake is discovered, its subsequent treatment and its individual genetic make-up than to the temperament of the species as a whole. The time of year and the stage in its shedding cycle may also be factors.

Even so, it is worth noting the species that have especially 'good' or 'bad' reputations. High on the list of species that are quick to react are the eastern and western diamondbacks (*Crotalus adamanteus* and *C. atrox*). The speckled rattlesnake (*C. mitchellii*) also has a bad reputation, as do some forms of the western rattlesnake (*C. viridis*). At the other end of the scale, the red diamond rattlesnake (*C. ruber*) is often said to be the most peaceful and it can be difficult to provoke this species to rattle in the field (strangely, the San Lucas rattlesnake, which is either a colour form or a subspecies of the red diamond rattler, can be quite aggressive). In my own experience, I have found that some of the smaller species, such as the rock rattlesnake (*C. lepidus*), the sidewinder (*C. cerastes*) and the pygmy rattler (*Sistrurus miliarius*), are especially quick to defend themselves. The Cedros Island rattlesnake (*Crotalus exsul*), the black-tailed rattlesnake (*C. molossus*) and the tiger rattler (*C. tigris*) on the other hand seem placid. Several other species have been encountered only under captive conditions or have varied too much between individuals for a reliable impression to be formed.

To illustrate the unpredictability that can exist within a single species, the western diamondback, photographed in Arizona (page 101), sounded off when first disturbed but then settled down almost immediately and allowed me to approach to within less than a metre to take wide-angled photographs. By contrast, an example of the same species photographed on Isla San Pedro Martir (page 60) rattled continuously for about half an hour, hissing, lunging and striking every time I made the slightest movement.

Reproduction

All rattlesnakes give birth to live young, as do most other vipers. Variation between species is limited to litter size and to the seasonal pattern of reproduction. A number of studies have looked at this aspect of their lives and, although there is still plenty to learn, they have produced some interesting information. As usual, the commoner, northern species are much better known than the rarer and less accessible Mexican ones.

Reproductive seasons and cycles

The two important annual events in every rattlesnake's calendar are mating and birth. Having said this, some female rattlesnakes take a year off and breed only every other year. Some may even rest for two years if the food supply is poor.

The female reproductive cycle

Mating can take place in the spring, summer or autumn, depending on the species and its location. Species that mate in the spring, mainly the lowland desert ones, may mate again in the autumn. Other species mate in the summer only. Spring matings lead to birth of the young in the late summer of the same year. Autumn and summer matings produce offspring the following year. This is possible only through the phenomenon of sperm storage, which is common in snakes, especially vipers.

Sperm storage allows two reproductive events – mating and birth – to be disconnected. Both can take place at the most convenient time of the year, independent of one another. Among the higher animals, this system is unique to reptiles. In females, mating is followed by ovulation – the releasing of the eggs cells, or ova, from the ovaries. Ovulation may occur shortly after mating, as in species that mate in the spring, or some time afterwards, as in species that mate in the summer and autumn. When ovulation is delayed the sperm is stored in a special chamber at the bottom of the oviduct. The amount of time it remains there depends on the species and its breeding system. Montane species, such as the ridge-nosed rattlesnake, for example, store sperm from one summer right through to the following spring.

Once ovulation occurs, the sperm fertilizes each egg and development of the young rattlesnakes begins. The female spends as much time as possible basking in order to speed up the development of the young. This is one advantage of bearing live young – the female has more control over the temperature of the developing offspring than she would if she laid eggs. At certain times of the year, female rattlesnakes are more likely to be seen than males because they spend more time basking on the surface. The pregnant females of some species, such as the prairie rattlesnake, congregate in special areas known as 'rookeries'. These places are probably attractive to females because they are warmer than the surrounding areas.

Female rattlesnakes give birth at the end of the summer. In the northern hemisphere this may be any time from August to October, depending on where they live. Not much is known about the birth, but it probably takes only two or three hours altogether. The young are each enclosed in a thin transparent membrane from which they escape within minutes of being born. Although they may stay near their place of birth for a few days, they soon disperse and, as far as anybody knows, they have little future contact with their mother or their littermates. Young rattlesnakes are more or less identical to their parents except that they lack a rattle until they have shed their skin a few times. Their markings may be slightly brighter but there are no major colour changes as they mature, as there are in some other species of snakes.

By the time they reach maturity, three or four years later, they may have spread out over a large area if the habitat is continuous. In more restrictive habitats, however, such as talus slides or montane meadows, the population may well consist of related individuals. Snakes' inability to migrate over long distances probably means that some degree of inbreeding is inevitable.

The male reproductive cycle

In terms of biological investment, the male's contribution towards the next generation – the sperm – is far less costly than the eggs of the female. Males produce their sperm during their most active period, in the summer, regardless of when they mate. If necessary, they store it until it is required.

The high point of every reproductive male's year is mating, which, as we have seen, may occur during almost any month from early spring through to late autumn. It is important for each male to mate with as many females as possible in order to ensure the maximum inheritance of his genes. Competition for females can be intense and has led to the evolution of ritualized combat behaviour between mature males at mating time. Males find females by following trails of pheromones, chemicals that the females leave as they move around (like perfume). Several males can follow the same pheromone trail and find the same female. They may have to wait a few days before the female is receptive and they spend this time fighting over the right to mate with her.

During combat 'dances' the males rear up together with the front parts of their bodies intertwined, each trying to force the other to the ground. They do not bite or otherwise harm each other, but bouts may go on for several hours, with frequent rests while the opponents gather their strength. Eventually one male will concede defeat and make off. The other may chase him for a short distance but soon returns to the side of the female, and may mate with her.

This kind of direct competition between male rattlesnakes has led to the natural selection of larger males. Large males are the ones most likely to win in combat and so get the chance to pass on their genes to the next generation. In this way, genes for large males spread throughout the population. There is also selective pressure on females to grow large (because large females can produce more young); this pressure must be less, however, because female rattlesnakes are, with one exception, always smaller than the males of the same species. The single exception is the sidewinder. Male sidewinders are smaller than females, probably because they do not fight and there is therefore no selective pressure on them to grow larger.

MATING

When they mate, the male snake crawls along the female's back, rubbing her with his chin to stimulate her. He also wraps his tail around hers and tries to bring their cloacae together. If the female is receptive she will lift her tail and allow him to couple. The male has paired reproductive organs, called hemipenes, normally retracted into pockets at the base of his tail. He only uses one to mate. The snakes may remain joined for several hours and, if one or the other decides to move, the other is dragged along behind.

Each female may mate several times over a period of a few days, either with the same male or, given the opportunity, with several different males. In this way she obtains a good selection of genes for her young and increases the chances that at least some of them will be fit enough to survive.

BIRTH

The number of young in the litter may vary from one to more than 20, with an average somewhere between 6 and 10. Larger species tend to have larger litters and the size of each young might also be larger. This also holds true within species: larger individuals have bigger litters than small ones.

The number and size of young that each female produces is sometimes compared with the size of the female and is called her reproductive effort. The reproductive effort of most snakes is, on average, about 25 per cent – this means that the litter (or clutch, in the case of egg-laying snakes) weighs about 25 per cent of the weight of the mother. Reproductive effort in live-bearing snakes is typically less than it is in egg-layers, probably because these snakes have additional costs to bear, like that of carrying their young for a longer time and being prevented from feeding in the latter stages of pregnancy.

Rattlesnake litters are born in late summer and early autumn. In the northern hemisphere this is from August to October, with September being the month in which most females give birth. Because fertilization may take place some time after mating, the gestation period can be difficult to estimate. It is probably about four to six months in most species, but there will be variations from place to place and from year to year, depending on the weather.

Most of what has been said here about mating seasons, development, etc. applies to rattlesnakes in North America, where there is a definite summer and winter. The habits of tropical rattlesnakes are poorly known, but it is likely that they also have predictable cycles, perhaps linked to wet and dry seasons rather than hot and cold ones. Captive rattlesnakes from tropical and sub-tropical climes may give birth at almost any time of the year, although spring and early summer seem to be most common. The Urocoan rattlesnake (*Crotalus durissus vegrandis*), which is widely bred in captivity, can produce a litter of young every nine months, but this is unlikely to occur under natural circumstances.

LONGEVITY

In the wild, rattlesnakes' lives are often cut short by predation, diseases or accidents. It is difficult to know how long they can live under these circumstances. In addition, species that hibernate for long periods each year probably live longer than those that are active all year long because they go into a type of suspended animation during which time they probably do not age. Their life-span, in real terms, is difficult to calculate. Records of rattlesnakes that have been kept in captivity give us some idea of their potential life-span. Some species are rarely kept in captivity, however, and our knowledge of them is incomplete.

We do know that some species, such as the western diamondback rattlesnake, can live for over 30 years, and plenty of species have lived for between 10 and 20 years. Male rattlesnakes probably mature at about four years, females at four to six years under natural circumstances. Even allowing for biennial breeding, females are probably capable of producing a minimum of about six litters of young during their lifetimes.

3

ORIGINS AND EVOLUTION

Rattlesnakes did not just suddenly appear, they evolved. Because they are a well-defined group of snakes, with obvious affinities with other well-defined groups, we can, up to a point, work out their origins and relationships, both with each other and with other snakes. To do this we need to know when they first appeared, where they came from and their degree of 'relatedness' to each other and to the vipers.

Fossil rattlesnakes

Rattlesnakes are among the most recently evolved snakes. The earliest fossils date from about five million years ago, at the most, and may only be four million years old. By comparison, the oldest snake fossils were found in deposits that were laid down in the Cretaceous period, 100–140 million years ago. Fossils from related species, other vipers, have been found to be about 22–30 million years old, and very closely related species, other American pit vipers, about 10 million years old. This gives us a rough time frame.

Rattlesnake fossils occur in many parts of the United States but are especially frequent in places where rattlesnakes are still quite common and in which the geology of the land lends itself, firstly, to the formation of fossils and, secondly, to their excavation at the present time. They are, for example, particularly numerous in Florida, which meets both these requirements. Many rattlesnakes fossils are not very old and belong to the identical species that are living today. Others are clearly extinct species and two of these have been named: *Crotalus potterensis* from California, and *C. giganteus* from Florida.

Like several other island forms, the San Esteban black-tailed rattlesnake, Crotalus molossus estebanensis, *is in the process of losing its rattle. Island species and subspecies are subject to different evolutionary pressures from those living on the mainland.*

Origins of the rattlesnakes

The rattlesnakes' closest relatives are other pit vipers, which are found in North and South America and in Asia (one species also enters Europe, but only just). As we have already seen, they are distinguished from other vipers by their heat-sensitive facial pits. The viper family, or Viperidae, is quite large, with about 200 species, and is found throughout Europe and Africa as well as Asia and the Americas. None of its members occurs in Australia or Madagascar, however, and the general opinion is that vipers were not able to colonize these regions because they had not evolved by the time they split away from the main landmasses.

Vipers originated in Asia and spread out from there into Europe and Africa. One line of Asiatic vipers developed the facial pits that distinguish them from other vipers and evolved into the pit vipers. At various times during the earth's history, north-east Asia was connected to north-west America by a landbridge situated where the Bering Strait is now. Many animals, including humans, have used this corridor to disperse from the Old World to the New, and pit vipers were among them (Fig. 7). The current view is that, having reached north-west America, the early pit vipers gradually spread

Fig. 7 *Pit vipers probably evolved in Asia, then spread eastwards, into north-western America and down into Mexico, which appears to have been a centre of evolution for rattlesnakes. From here, they spread into other parts of North America and one species,* Crotalus durissus, *spread south, into South America.*

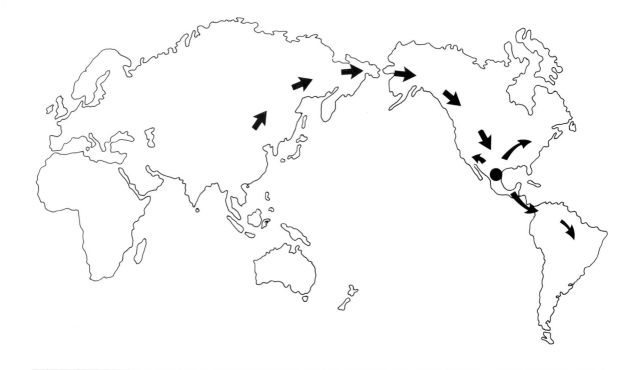

southwards, probably due to progressively worsening climatic conditions in the north, and eventually reached Mexico. There they underwent a good deal of speciation – they moved into different types of habitats and adapted accordingly.

At some point along the way, the rattle evolved in one line of pit vipers, and this line gave rise to the two genera of rattlesnakes, *Crotalus* and *Sistrurus*. As conditions improved, the pit vipers, including the ones that had evolved into rattlesnakes, radiated out again, to colonize most of North America as well as parts of Central and South America. As they spread, they continued to evolve into additional species and subspecies. Some species later became extinct, perhaps after they had given rise to other, better adapted species. Others may have been evolutionary dead ends.

The pygmy rattlesnakes, belonging to the genus *Sistrurus*, are thought to be the more primitive line, because the arrangement of their head scales is similar to that of the ancestral line of pit vipers. The other rattlesnakes, *Crotalus*, must have evolved from snakes similar to modern day *Sistrurus* species.

ISLAND SPECIES

Because of their isolation, island populations can often tell us more about the spread and evolution of animals than can mainland populations. Rattlesnakes occur on a number of islands, including one or two in the Caribbean, but the most interesting are those in the Gulf of California, where there are a good number of rattlesnake species and subspecies (Fig. 8). Briefly, it seems that rattlesnakes could have reached these islands in one of three ways. They could have already been on the islands when their connection with the mainland was broken by rising sea-levels; they could have swum to the islands; or they could have arrived as stowaways on driftwood or other floating debris. It seems that the species and subspecies found on islands are most closely related to the species and subspecies found on adjacent parts of the mainland. This leads us to believe that they were already on some of the islands when they became separated. Some islands are volcanic in origin, however, and the rattlesnakes on them must have arrived by another method.

There are 28 reasonably large islands in the Gulf, 17 of which have rattlesnakes on them. Two islands have three species of rattler and five islands have two. Two species, the Santa Catalina rattleless rattlesnake (*Crotalus catalinensis*) and the Tortuga Island rattlesnake (*C. tortugensis*), are unique to their islands and are not found on the

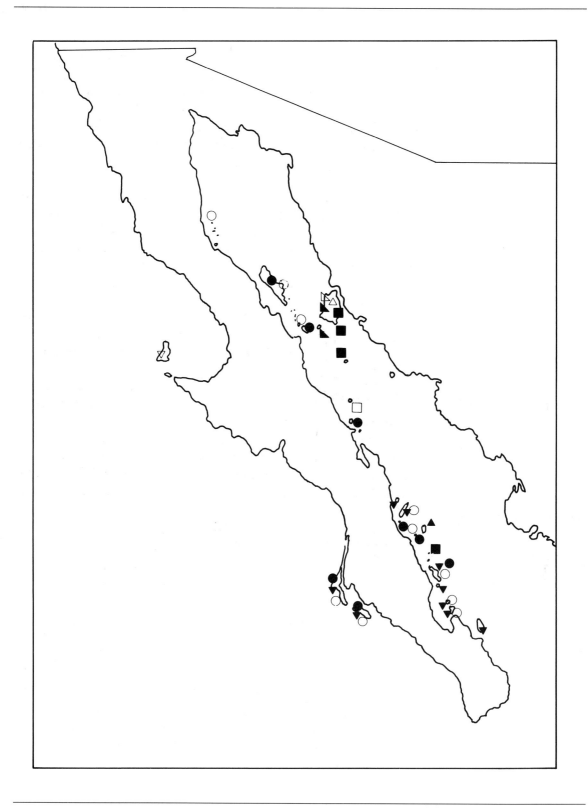

mainland. All the islands are dry, rocky and barren, none of them is permanently inhabited by humans, and they all have an impoverished flora and fauna. Compared with the mainland, where the living is relatively easy, animals arriving on the islands must find ways of coping with the adverse conditions – they must adapt or die.

Some rattlesnakes evolved in novel ways once they reached their islands. The speckled rattlesnakes (*C. mitchellii*), on the island of Angel de la Guarda, for instance, grow much larger than their mainland relatives – to more than 130cm (51in), compared with 100cm (39in) on the mainland. Interestingly, the population of the same species on another island, El Muerto, stayed smaller than average, never exceeding 70cm (27in). *C. catalinensis* also remains smaller than its mainland relatives, but it is even more remarkable for the loss of its rattle. Its rattle matrix – the part of the tail that grips the segments – is so small that new segments fall off almost as soon as they are formed. Two other island forms also seem to be in the process of losing their rattles. These are the San Esteban black-tailed rattlesnake (*C. molossus estebanensis*) and the San Lorenzo red diamond rattlesnake (*C. ruber lorenzoensis*).

Gigantism and dwarfism are characteristics of island populations of a variety of other animals – the giant tortoises of the Galapagos are an example. One theory is that dwarf species evolve because they can manage with less food. Large species evolve, paradoxically, for similar reasons; food may be abundant at certain times of the year but is then absent. Large animals can store more food, in the form

Fig. 8 Opposite: *Rattlesnakes are distributed throughout the islands in the Gulf of California and those off the Pacific coast of Baja California – some must have reached the islands hundreds of thousands of years ago and have evolved into unique species or subspecies whereas others are more recent invaders from adjacent parts of the mainland of Mexico or the peninsula of Baja California.*

KEY

- ■ *Crotalus atrox* (Tiburón, Dátil, San Pedro Martir, Santa Cruz)
- ▲ *C. catalinensis* (Santa Catalina – endemic)
- △ *C. cerastes* (Tiburón – subspecies *C. cerastes cercombobus*)
- ▼ *C. enyo* (Carmen, Coronados, Espíritu Santo, Magdalena, Partida Sur, San Francisco, San José, Santa Margarita – subspecies *C. enyo enyo*; Cerralvo – subspecies *C. enyo cerralvensis*)
- ▼ *C. exsul* (Cedros)
- ○ *C. mitchellii* (Carmen, Cerralvo, Espíritu Santo, Magdalena, Monserrate, Partida Sur, Piojo, Salsipuedes, San José, Santa Margarita, Smith – subspecies *C. mitchellii mitchellii*; Angel de la Guarda – subspecies *C. mitchellii angelensis*; El Muerto – subspecies *C. mitchellii muertensis*; Salsipuedes – subspecies *C. mitchellii pyrrhus*)
- ◣ *C. molossus* (Tiburón – subspecies *C. molossus molossus*; San Esteban – subspecies *C. molossus estebanensis*)
- ● *C. ruber* (Angel de la Guarda, San Marcos, Magdalena, Santa Margarita – subspecies *C. ruber ruber*; San Lorenzo Sur – subspecies *C. ruber lorenzoensis*; Monserrate, San José, Danzante – subspecies *C. ruber lucasensis*)
- ◁ *C. tigris* (Tiburón)
- □ *C. tortugensis* (Tortuga – endemic)

of fat, than small ones can. The Chappell Island tiger snakes, off the coast of Australia, for instance, are larger than the mainland form because they feed heavily on the chicks of mutton birds, which are available for only a limited season. If it could be shown that the rattlesnakes on Angel de la Guarda fed heavily on nesting seabirds during the spring, but that those of El Muerte had no such food supply, this would be a tidy explanation of their differences in size. But, until someone looks into this, we will have to speculate.

The other evolutionary quirk, rattle loss, is more enigmatic. It has been suggested that some of the island rattlesnakes have had to change from a diet of terrestrial rodents to one of birds and lizards, climbing into bushes while they are roosting at night. If this is correct, the rattle may have become more of a hindrance than a help. Natural selection will have favoured the snakes with smaller, less noisy and less cumbersome rattles. Then again, the rattle may have shrunk because, like the human appendix, it was no longer needed: after all, there are no large animals to trample rattlesnakes on these small desert islands.

A FAMILY TREE

All rattlesnakes are related, but some are more related than others. Closely related species are the ones that were separated from one another quite recently, whereas distantly related ones have been separated for much longer. By looking in detail at anatomical structures and at the proteins in rattlesnakes' blood and venom, researchers can produce a 'family tree' of rattlesnakes.

The most obvious divergence is between the rattlesnakes placed in the genus *Sistrurus* (the massassauga, the pygmy rattlesnake and the Mexican pygmy rattlesnake) and the other species, which are placed in the genus *Crotalus*. The most important difference between these two genera is the arrangement of the head scales – nine large, plate-like, scales in the case of *Sistrurus* and many small, fragmented scales in the case of *Crotalus*. Rattlesnake ancestors had large head scales, like *Sistrurus*, so the small, fragmented head scales of the *Crotalus* species must have evolved after the split – *Sistrurus* are the more primitive species.

Within *Crotalus*, a number of groups are recognizable, containing similar species. *C. basiliscus* and *C. molossus* are very closely related to

Crotalus catalinensis *has no rattle. Its rattle matrix is misshapen so that subsequent segments fall off as soon as they are formed.*

76

each other, as are *C. atrox*, *C. exsul* and *C. ruber*. Other closely related groups can also be recognized. The species that seems to be least related to any others is the timber rattlesnake, *C. horridus*.

How rattlesnakes may have evolved

Like other animals, rattlesnakes have been shaped by a process of evolution that has gone on, and is still going on, in a seemingly random fashion. Evolution has no target, no end product, but makes relentless progress by fine-tuning populations of animals to fit into the environment in which they live. Those that do not measure up to the challenge perish early and are unable to pass on their genes. As poor genes are eliminated, so good genes proliferate and spread throughout the population. All this happens so slowly that we are unable to see the changes, but changes have already taken place: what we observe now is the ghost of selection past – the surviving offspring of the surviving offspring, going way back to a time before the rattlesnakes' ancestors became rattlesnakes.

Because they all share a number of unique features, it is an interesting exercise to try and piece together and speculate on their evolutionary history. Rattlesnakes as a group are a fairly conservative set of species, by which we mean that they have, by and large, found a formula by which to survive and have stuck to it. The 30 or so species are remarkably similar in their general appearance and in their habits. For instance, they all give birth to live young – there are no exceptions. Similarly, they are all terrestrial snakes – there are no aquatic or arboreal species, and none of them burrow to any great extent. All this, together with the possession of a rattle and several other anatomical characteristics, point to a common ancestry.

In the absence of a time machine, the only way we can trace the course of events that culminated in rattlesnakes looking and behaving the way they do, is to undertake some fairly speculative detective work, using what we know about snakes' biology and behaviour to attempt to reconstruct the evolution of rattlesnakes, step by step.

Our starting point should be a fairly typical snake, not venomous, not too thick, not too thin and with a fairly standard set of senses and sense organs. It will have reproduced by laying eggs (because this is the primitive condition in snakes). There were plenty of snakes fitting this description in the Miocene era, which lasted from 22 to 5 million years ago, and, over time, they diversified in various directions to give rise to many of the ancestral lines that still exist. One of these lines gave rise to the rattlesnakes.

All living snakes are predatory and there is no reason to suppose that ancestral snakes were any different. Our 'typical' snake, then, ate other animals, and somewhere along the line it had an evolutionary choice to make in respect of its method of hunting. It could spend its time chasing after its prey, in which case it would need to be fast moving and, probably, active during the day; quite a number of snakes took this pathway. Alternatively, it could sit and wait for its prey to pass by and then ambush it. In this case, it would not need to move so fast and, indeed, the best shape for snakes that ambush their prey is short and fat. Their heavy bodies act as an anchor point while they throw their relatively light head forward when they strike. As a bonus, their bulky shape enables them to accommodate bigger prey, and this can be important to animals that rely on their meals coming to them and so cannot afford to be too choosy. Furthermore, because ambushers do not need to move quickly, having a large meal inside them is not such a burden as it would be in fast-moving snakes. This theory has been supported by scientific investigation – snakes that ambush their prey tend to eat larger meals than similarly sized snakes that actively chase their prey. A further implication is that snakes that ambush their prey need to be well camouflaged so that they can remain undetected by their prey. Already our snake is taking shape: it is bulky, with a small head and thick body, and well camouflaged – all a consequence of its choosing to wait for its prey rather than chase it.

The next stage may have been the evolution of venom and the apparatus with which to deliver it. Sit-and-wait predators are either powerful constrictors (such as the boas and pythons) or they are venomous. The reason is rather obvious – if they cannot chase after their prey, they must make sure of overpowering it at the first attempt. Furthermore, because the prey may be relatively large, as we have already seen, any means of subduing it quickly is likely to be advantageous; there is less likelihood of its inflicting injuries as it fights back. The venom must act quickly, and it must be capable of being delivered deep into the body of the prey, which may be covered in a thick layer of fur or feathers.

This leads to the evolution of long, hollow fangs, to penetrate the prey's body and deliver the venom where it is most effective – often the chest region. If necessary, the prey can then be released and tracked down later when the venom has taken effect. But these same long fangs that are so useful for capturing prey can also be something of a liability. Closing the mouth becomes hazardous and some means of folding them out of harm's way must be developed. This is done most effectively by hinging the part of the upper jaw to which they are attached.

So far, then, we have a group of snakes that are heavy-bodied, well camouflaged, with effective venom and long, hinged fangs. This definition fits the vipers very well and we can suppose that they, or snakes very like them, had arrived on the scene.

There is even an added bonus. Because these snakes were large, relied on camouflage and were well able to defend themselves, they were able to improve on their ancestral reproductive habits. Instead of releasing their eggs at an early stage in their development, they could retain them within their body and carry them around without suffering the same disadvantages of snakes that relied entirely on speed to escape from predators. This meant they were able to bask in the sun to keep their offspring warm and so speed up their development. In addition, by defending themselves, they also defended their unborn young.

Now we need to look at another aspect of snakes' biology in order to find the key to further evolutionary progress. In particular, the activity patterns of our pioneering vipers will have been dependent on the prevailing climatic conditions. In cool regions they may have hunted during the day, perhaps lying among leaves or a jumble of rocks where their camouflage made them difficult to detect. In hot regions, though, they must have hunted at night, or in the early morning and late evening periods, to avoid the lethal daytime temperatures. This, of course, would enhance the benefit of their camouflage and help them to avoid detection but it would present them with a new problem – the difficulty of being able to see their prey once it came within range. They could detect its presence by their jawbones, which are sensitive to vibration, and by the olfactory part of the brain, where scent particles, picked up by the tongue and transferred to the Jacobson's organ, are analysed, but its exact position cannot be accurately established by these means. The answer, in the case of one group of vipers, was to evolve an additional and unique sense organ, the heat pits in their face. These enabled them to pinpoint the exact position of a warm animal, even in total darkness. It is these organs that separate the pit vipers from the typical, or Old World, vipers.

Vipers the world over, including this young Lataste's viper, Vipera latasti, *from central Spain, tend to be stocky, and have small heads and keeled scales. Rattlesnakes inherited all these characteristics.*

Our snake, then, has come a long way from the typical, slender, non-venomous creature without any special sense organs. There are, however, still further refinements that can be made. In making itself almost invisible, either because it is perfectly camouflaged or because it is active at night, it has, to some extent, created a fresh problem for itself. With the appearance of large four-footed animals, the danger of being trampled becomes a distinct possibility and so some way of avoiding this unhappy end has to be found. Again, there are several possible solutions. Some snakes developed the habit of hissing loudly in order to warn their potental enemies, and a few, such as the saw-scaled vipers from Africa and Asia, evolved specialized scales on their flanks that they could rub together to produce a loud rasping sound. Others, though, by some freak of mutation, evolved an organ on the end of their tail which, when vibrated, produced a loud and unmistakable sound, nature's answer to the bicycle bell, car hooter or police siren – the rattle.

Not all pit vipers have a rattle because some lines had already begun to evolve in other directions by the time it appeared. Perhaps they lived in areas where there were no large animals or perhaps they would have benefited from a rattle but had to manage without. Whichever was the case, the story of the rattlesnake seems to have begun with what may have seemed to be a fairly straightforward 'choice' early on – whether to go chasing after prey or whether to wait for it to come to them. Once they had made that decision, the die was cast and the appearance of the other characteristics that make them rattlesnakes seems to have followed a logical sequence.

The evolutionary pathway can be summarized like this:

- Development of a sit-and-wait method of hunting leads to a large body, small head and camouflage.

- This leads to the potential to eat large prey and the need to kill quickly and the evolution of venom and long, hinged fangs. The possibility of giving birth to live young is available.

  → Vipers

- Life in a hot environment leads to a nocturnal activity pattern, which leads to evolution of the pits.

  → Pit vipers

- The risk of being trampled leads to evolution of the rattle.

  → Rattlesnakes

Early American pit vipers, of which the copperhead, Agkistrodon contortrix, *is a modern example, gave rise to the rattlesnakes. The first pit vipers, however, originated in Asia.*

4

INTERACTIONS WITH HUMANS

Few animals interact more dramatically with us than venomous snakes. Rattlesnakes and people have been killing each other since the human race first arrived in North America. Yet the battle has probably always been one-sided – we do more of the attacking than they do. Even so, 'man versus snake' is never quite as newsworthy as 'snake versus man', and what people most want to know about rattlesnakes is how dangerous they are.

Snake bite

Although we have already dealt with why rattlesnakes bite, and with the evolution of venom and its effects (see Chapter 3), snake bite of humans warrants a separate discussion.

There are several factors that affect the likelihood of being bitten, the most important of which appear to be location, time of day, and the age and occupation of the victim. Location is important from two angles: some areas have more rattlesnakes than others and some have more people than others. Where the human population is dense, their distribution over the land will also be important, because a large rural population will be more vulnerable that a large urban one.

If you are determined not to be bitten by a rattlesnake in America, my advice would be to live in Alaska, Maine or Delaware because the chances of receiving a fatal bite from a wild rattlesnake are nil. There are no rattlesnakes in these states. (A small number of bites have been recorded in Delaware even though it has no rattlesnakes – presumably captive snakes were responsible.) The states with the greatest numbers of snake bites per capita are all southern and south-

Populations of the canebrake and timber rattlesnakes, Crotalus horridus horridus *and* C. h. atricaudatus *(illustrated), have shown an alarming decline in recent years. Both subspecies occur in the eastern United States and suffer from encroaching urban and agricultural development.*

eastern: North Carolina, Arkansas, Texas, Georgia, West Virginia, Mississippi and Louisiana, in descending order. Even so, the riskiest state, North Carolina, has an incidence of only about 19 bites per 100,000 head of population per year. This figure includes all bites, not just fatal ones, which would be a much smaller one.[3] Furthermore, these figures are over 30 years old and the chances of being bitten have declined since then and continue to do so.

Initially, it is something of a surprise to find that the south-western states, usually strongly associated with rattlers, have a low incidence of bites: 7 to 8 cases per 100,000 head of population per year in Arizona and New Mexico and 1½ cases per 100,000 in California. The reason behind this brings us on to the second relevant factor – occupation. It seems that the chances of being bitten are highest for people involved in agricultural activities. This is just what we would expect, so the states with a high proportion of agricultural workers are the ones where people get bitten most. Arizona, New Mexico and California have relatively small agricultural populations, high degrees of mechanization and, furthermore, farm workers and rattlesnakes have little contact in these states because they are active at different times of the day (the snakes are largely nocturnal for most of the year).

There might also be a correlation between victims' ages and snakebite but different surveys have given conflicting results. Most of them show that people between 20 and 30 years of age are most likely to be bitten and those between 1 and 10 are least likely.[4] Other studies, though, have shown that young children and older people are more vulnerable. What *is* certain is that children and older people are more likely to die if they do get bitten. Boys and men are more likely to be fatally bitten than girls and women, regardless of age. The location of the bite on the body is also relevant; bites to the head and torso (fortunately rare) are more serious than those on limbs, which are the most common targets.

Most bites occur in the spring and summer, when the snakes are most active. The activity patterns of people also have a bearing, with most bites occurring in the morning, afternoon and evening. Midnight to 6 a.m. is the time when fewest people are bitten. No surprises here.

3. H. M. Parrish, 1963, 'Incidence of treated snakebites in the United States', *Public Health Report*, 81:269.

4. F. E. Russell, 1979, 'The clinical problem of crotalid snake venom poisoning', in Lee, C. Y. (ed.), *Handbook of Experimental Pharmacology, Snake Venoms*, vol. 52:978, Springer Verlag, Berlin.

So, you are most likely to get bitten if you are a man in your 20s living in one of the south-eastern states and working on the land. Even then, the risks of a fatal bite are so small that they hardly exist at all.

To put this into perspective, the likelihood of dying because of a rattlesnake bite in the United States is less than that of being hit by lightning and many orders of magnitude less than being killed in an automobile accident. Remember, the chances of being bitten are going down all the time. For those who do get bitten, the fatality rate is going down too, due to improved medical facilities, improved telecommunications and the availability of road and air transport, even from quite remote areas.

On the other hand, the chances of being bitten are dramatically above average for people who keep rattlesnakes in captivity, go out of their way to hunt them or put on heroic performances when they come across them. Young men in their 20s and 30s are, again, the most likely victims. Bites brought about by activities such as these are known, rather quaintly, as 'illegitimate' as opposed to accidental bites, which are 'legitimate'.

Myths and studies

EARLY WRITERS

The first North Americans almost certainly arrived by the same route as the rattlesnakes, via the land bridge that existed where the Bering Strait is now. Although these people will have come into contact with rattlesnakes, our account of man's interaction with them starts much later than this, after Columbus's discovery of the New World.

The first Europeans to encounter rattlesnakes, then, were the Portuguese and Spanish explorers who gradually spread out over the Americas. Because these adventurers first reached the shores of South and Central America, many of the early accounts refer to the neotropical species, now known as *Crotalus durissus*. The earliest written account is probably that of Pedro de Cieça de Leon, in *La Chronica del Peru*, published in 1554. In it he describes the sound made by the rattle as that of bells and points out that the bite can be lethal. The first published illustration of a rattlesnake was by Francisco Hernandez in 1628.[5] It accompanied an article (also

5. Francisco Hernandez, 1628, *Rerum Medicarum Novae Hispaniae Thesaurus seu Plantarum Animalium Mineralium Mexicanorum Historia*.

published earlier without the illustration) in which he described the defensive behaviour of rattlesnakes, their black eyes and hollow fangs and numerous other details, some of which were accurate and some mythical. He also pointed out that there was more than one kind of rattlesnake.

By the early seventeenth century references were being made to rattlesnakes in English. Some of these were translations from earlier Spanish manuscripts and contained the same errors. Others were more accurate and several included the term 'rattlesnake' in one form or another. Thomas Morton, for example, writing in 1637, says: 'There is one creeping beast . . . that hath a rattle in his tayle, that doth discover his age; for so many years as hee hath lived, so many joynts are in that rattle, which soundeth (when it is in motion) like pease in a bladder, and this beast is called a rattlesnake.'[6] Note how he refers to the old belief that rattlesnakes' ages could be told by the number of segments in their rattles, and how well he describes the sound they produce.

In subsequent years, references to rattlesnakes were frequent as settlers moved into new areas, but much of this information was hearsay, inaccurate or downright fanciful. The first accurate account of the rattlesnake's anatomy was written by Tyson. It was published in 1682[7] and has an early reference to the facial pits. In 1727 Captain Hall experimented with dogs to show that rattlesnakes eventually exhausted their supply of venom if they bit repeatedly. Subsequently, many authors made small but important contributions to the natural history of rattlesnakes, often with emphasis on the formation and function of the rattle or on the effects of the bite.

SOME EARLY MYTHS

Myths about rattlesnakes take many forms. Some of them arrived with Europeans and are transplants of similar myths surrounding European and African snakes. Others were home-grown in America. Klauber (see Further Reading, page 140) lists countless examples and variations, rattlesnake folklore being one of the main subjects of his study, but I can mention only a few here, concentrating mainly on those that relate specifically to rattlesnakes rather than snakes in general. Many are to do with the venom and snake bite and they include the following:

6 T. Morton, 1637, *New English Canaan* (quotation modified from Klauber, 1977).

7. E. Tyson, 1682, '*Vipera Caudisona Americana*, or the anatomy of a rattlesnake', *Philosophical Transactions of the Royal Society*, 13:25–28.

- If a rattlesnake is killed, anyone who it has bitten will recover immediately. Another version of the story says that if the person lives, the snake will die but if the person dies, the snake will live.

- If a drunk or sick man is bitten, the snake will die.

- Rattlesnakes will not bite children under the age of seven. Other stories explain that they will bite men but not women, will not bite while in the water or will not bite a person from behind.

- If a rattlesnake bites a tree, the tree will die. Furthermore, if a man is holding a branch that is bitten the venom will travel up the branch and affect the man.

- If a rattlesnake bites the wooden handle of a tool such as a hoe, the wood swells. (A similar fate befell the legendary character, Peg-leg Ike, whose wooden leg was bitten in a tongue-in-cheek story recorded in a journal dedicated to tall tales.)

- Rattlesnakes can hypnotize or charm their prey, especially birds, which subsequently walk into the snake's open mouth.

Then there are the supposed remedies that can be prepared from one part or another of a rattlesnake's anatomy, often its skin but also from the gall bladder, heart, liver and muscle. It would appear that the relevant preparations are effective against just about everything, from a headache to decapitation. A complete list of treatable diseases would read like a medical dictionary, but it includes toothache, rheumatism, epilepsy, sore throat and saddle sores. Necklaces of rattlesnake vertebrae are recommended for epilepsy, chills and fevers (such necklaces can still be bought in parts of Mexico). Perhaps the most imaginative cures involved drowning the rattlesnake in wine (for leprosy) or mixing its gall bladder with clay (for fevers and smallpox). Dried rattlesnake in corn whiskey sounds as though it may have been one of the more popular cures for rheumatism.

Ways of avoiding rattlesnake bites were equally imaginative. It was thought, for instance, that rattlesnakes would not cross a hair rope and so one would be used to encircle a campsite. Other repellents include ash wood and onions. Burning old shoes was thought to be effective in driving rattlesnakes away in parts of Arkansas and Pennsylvania. Having once burned some old shoes on a garden bonfire I am inclined to think that there may be some truth in this!

CLASSIFICATION

After the early explorers, interest in rattlesnakes took a more scientific turn. The field of herpetology (the study of reptiles and amphibians) grew quickly in the nineteenth century and produced many excellent and prolific workers. Although some of these made original observations about the behaviour and natural history of rattlesnakes, the main thrust of their work was to discover new species and classify them.

The binomial system of nomenclature, in which two latinized words are used to describe living organisms, did not appear until 1753 with Linnaeus' *Species Plantarum*. More editions of this followed under the title of *Systema Naturae* in an attempt to name all living organisms known at the time, including snakes. The first three rattlesnakes were named in 1758, in the 10th edition. These are *Crotalus durissus*, *Crotalus horridus* and *Crotalus dryinas*. The name of the latter was changed to *Crotalus durissus terrificus*. In the 12th edition (in 1766) the first of the pygmy rattlesnakes, *Crotalus miliarius*, was named, although it was later changed to *Sistrurus miliarius*.

Following the naming of these species, there was a lull for over 40 years before the next species, *C. adamanteus*, was described in 1799. The nineteenth century, often known as the 'heyday of natural history', saw a flurry of biological exploration in the New World and a further 18 species (16 *Crotalus* and 2 *Sistrurus*) were described between 1824 and 1895. The remaining 7 species (all *Crotalus*) have been described this century, with the most recent being *C. lannomi* in 1966.

The scientific names of the species, together with the dates they were first formally described and their authors, are summarized in the table opposite.

Thankfully, rattlesnakes have a fairly stable nomenclature. Unlike many other groups of snakes, there has been little 'tinkering' with their names in recent years. One doubtful form that is easily dealt with is *Crotalus unicolor*, the Aruba Island rattlesnake, which, though recognized as a full species by many authorities, is considered to be a subspecies of *Crotalus durissus* by others. Although this may seem to be a minor point, it has some relevance within the field of conservation because this is one of the rarer rattlesnakes whose existence is threatened. It is the subject of a successful and ongoing captive breeding programme involving several North American zoos.

Date	Species	Author and notes
1758	*Crotalus durissus*	Linnaeus
1758	*C. horridus*	Linnaeus
1766	*Sistrurus miliarius*	Linneaus (as *Crotalus miliarius*)
1799	*C. adamanteus*	Beauvois
1818	*C. viridis*	Rafinesque
1818	*S. catenatus*	Rafinesque (as *Crotalinus catenatus*)
1830	*C. triseriatus*	Wagler (as *Uropsophus triseriatus*)
1853	*C. atrox*	Baird and Girard
1853	*C. molossus*	Baird and Girard
1854	*C. cerastes*	Hallowell
1859	*C. polystictus*	Cope (as *Crotalus lugubris* (part))
1859	*C. tigris*	Kennicott
1861	*C. enyo*	Cope
1861	*C. lepidus*	Kennicott (as *Caudisona lepidus*)
1861	*C. mitchellii*	Cope (as *Caudisona mitchellii*)
1861	*C. scutulatus*	Kennicott (as *Caudisona scutulatus*)
1865	*C. basiliscus*	Cope (as *Caudisona basiliscus*)
1865	*S. ravus*	Cope (as *Crotalus ravus*)
1866	*C. intermedius*	Troschel
1883	*C. exsul*	Garman
1887	*C. unicolor**	van Lithe de Jeude (as *C. horridus unicolor*)
1892	*C. ruber*	Cope (as *C. adamanteus ruber*)
1895	*C. pricei*	Van Denburgh
1906	*C. willardi*	Meek
1919	*C. stejnegeri*	Dunn
1921	*C. tortugensis*	Van Denburgh and Slevin
1944	*C. transversus*	Taylor
1952	*C. pusillus*	Klauber
1954	*C. catalinensis*	Cliff
1966	*C. lannomi*	Tanner
1992	*C. aquilus*	Dorcas

* *C. unicolor* is usually regarded as a subspecies of *C. durissus*, *C. durissus unicolor*.

The status of some of the island forms from the Gulf of California have also been brought into question recently, especially *Crotalus exsul* and *C. ruber*. This is a more complicated matter, and somewhat irrelevant to the general naturalist, so I have dealt with it elsewhere in the form of a short note (page 109, Chapter 5).

OTHER RESEARCH

Classification is only one aspect of rattlesnake research. Numerous workers have studied venom from different angles – to find effective ways of treating snakebite, and also to find out whether it has possible beneficial properties. Others have looked at ecological aspects – growth rates, population structures, how rattlesnakes interact with other organisms with which they share their habitats and how resources are shared among them.

Behavioural studies of all snakes have been difficult until recently, but the development of miniaturized telemetry systems for locating and tracking free-ranging snakes has revolutionized field studies of this kind and several rattlesnake projects are in progress. Results from some of these studies have already shown that rattlesnakes' lives are far more complex (and therefore interesting) than many of us had realized.

Conservation

Many species of snakes are hunted. Some have valuable skins, while others are eaten, used in medicinal preparations (modern or traditional) or sold as pets.

Although many kinds of snakes, venomous or otherwise, are likely to be killed if they are encountered by humans, rattlesnakes are, to the best of my knowledge, unique in having been the subject of a relentless persecution campaign, in the form of rattlesnake roundups. These events, which still take place in a few southern states, are designed specifically to exterminate rattlesnakes. Although in the past there may have been some justification for killing rattlesnakes, where they may have posed a threat to settlers and their livestock, this reason no longer exists. The amount of damage that is done to rattlesnake populations and to other animals that share their habitats is impossible to calculate.

In addition to organized roundups, there is a general feeling among motorists that snakes on the road are fair game, even if it involves swerving across the carriageway to hit them. A night-time drive along a desert road will often reveal the extent of the slaughter, although the evidence has often gone by morning, after scavenging birds and mammals have cleared away the carcasses. For many rattlesnakes living near a busy road, the grim reaper drives a saloon or pickup. The death toll must run into tens of thousands each year.

The speckled rattlesnake,
Crotalus mitchellii mitchellii.

They have little defence against a determined attack by a human, especially one who uses weapons such as clubs, firearms and motor cars. Humans affect rattlesnakes in many other ways, all of them negative. Apart from wanton killing, we destroy their habitat and reduce their food supply through agriculture and urban development, and the use of chemicals on the land. Rare species are sometimes collected for the pet trade or for zoos or museums.

I have shown (I hope) that rattlesnakes have a place in the scheme of things. They are beautifully adapted to the places they live in and are an interesting, if sometimes awesome, part of American culture and folklore. They are highly effective and mobile pest controllers. Occasionally they bite people but usually because they have been provoked.

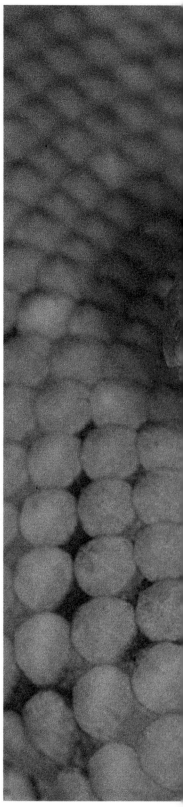

Irrespective, though, of their costs and benefits to us, rattlesnakes have the same right to exist as other animals. They have no need to prove their worth or justify their own existence. Even so, rattlesnake conservation is hardly likely to become a key issue in the near future. A few rare species, such as the Arizona ridge-nosed rattlesnake, are protected from collectors. Some species and subspecies have a limited degree of protection by virtue of their occurrence inside National Parks and other protected places. In some cases, though, rattlesnake populations can decline even in areas that are set aside for other rare animals. Richard Seigel's study, which has been mentioned earlier in connection with the activity patterns and feeding habits of massassaugas (see page 42), showed that even in a wildlife reserve, management practices such as burning of the prairie and the unrestricted access by people in motor cars had a detrimental effect on the rattlesnakes. This is made all the more worrying because this particular species has also been hard hit due to the draining of bogs in the northern parts of its range and the conversion of grasslands to grazing in southern parts.

Pressures on rattlesnakes are greatest in densely populated areas. Sometimes a species can be exterminated in one region and still remain common in another. At other times, a species' entire range coincides with the places where people want to live and work. The timber rattlesnake is one such species and there is concern for its survival in many of the areas where it was once common.

Of the many Mexican rattlesnakes, very little is known about their status. The inaccessibility of many montane habitats and low-tech agriculture probably help to lessen the human impact on them, but at least one species, *Crotalus polystictus*, has become rare since the meadows it favours have become cleared for agriculture.[8] Rattlesnakes as a whole are not threatened, but some of the more unusual species are becoming alarmingly rare and some of the more widespread species are no longer seen in places where they were formerly common.

8. H. W. Greene and J. A. Campbell, 1992, 'The future of pit vipers', in *The Biology of the Pit Vipers*, eds. J. A. Campbell, and E. D. Brodie, Selva, Tyler, Texas.

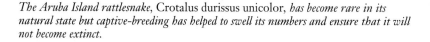

The Aruba Island rattlesnake, Crotalus durissus unicolor, *has become rare in its natural state but captive-breeding has helped to swell its numbers and ensure that it will not become extinct.*

5

RATTLESNAKE SPECIES

The following chapter contains a list of all known rattlesnakes, with a brief description of each and some notes about their distribution, habitats and their venoms.

Although the identification of rattlesnakes as a group could hardly be easier, distinguishing between the species can be difficult. Their colours, for instance, are not usually consistent enough for identification. Most species show some variation and many have wildly differing coloration depending on where they live, often matching the colour of the sand, soil or rock on which they normally rest. When seen in the wild, their locality is often the most important aid to identification. Many areas have only one or two species present (see the distribution maps). In areas such as Arizona, where several species occur, it might be possible to pinpoint (or eliminate) some immediately because of obvious and characteristic features – the raised scales over the eyes of sidewinders, for instance, or the black and white rings around the tail of the western diamondback and Mojave rattlesnakes. Using a combination of these characteristics and a knowledge of the locality, it should be possible to identify most rattlesnakes reasonably easily. Habitat is another good clue – many species are quite specific in their preferences and will rarely, if ever, be seen away from their normal environment.

If a rattlesnake appears to defy identification and you are tempted to look a little more closely, *don't*. Practise on roadkills!

Genus *Crotalus*, rattlesnakes

This genus contains 27 species at present. They are characterized by a rattle on the end of their tail and numerous small scales covering the tops of their head. No other snake genus has this combination of

The Baja, or Lower California, rattlesnake, Crotalus enyo.

characteristics. Very young rattlesnakes may not have a fully formed rattle but will have a 'button' at the tip of their tail which is quite easy to make out. The so-called 'rattleless' rattlesnake from Santa Catalina island in the Gulf of California retains the first segment of its rattle even though subsequent segments drop off.

Collectively, members of this genus range from southern Canada to Argentina, and from below sea-level to over 4,000m (13,000ft) in elevation. Not surprisingly, they are to be found in a wide range of habitats. The venom produced by the different species in this genus is of several types and bites range from the painful but relatively innocuous to the lethal.

The species and subspecies are dealt with alphabetically by scientific name.

The rock rattlesnake,
Crotalus lepidus.

Crotalus adamanteus

Eastern diamondback rattlesnake

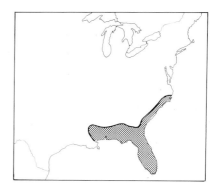

Description: the largest species of rattlesnake, normally growing to about 1.2–1.4m (4ft–4ft 8in), with exceptional specimens reaching 2m (6ft 6in) or more. It is grey or olive in colour, with well-defined, dark brown diamonds along its back. Each diamond is outlined with cream scales. Its head is mostly dark brown but two pale streaks pass obliquely down each side of its face, on either side of the eyes, and the eye stripe is very dark, often black. There are smaller, vertical pale streaks on the side of its snout.

Distribution (*see map*): south-eastern United States, including all of Florida, extreme south-eastern Louisiana (but now rare or extinct there) and the coastal plains of southern Mississippi, Alabama, Georgia, North Carolina and South Carolina.

Habitat: it is often associated with pine woods and palmetto scrub. Although much of the area over which it occurs consists of lowland swamp, eastern diamondbacks are most often found in raised, drier situations, where trees and shrubs grow. Having said this, it swims well, in fresh and salt water, and has been found several miles out to sea. It occurs on several of the Florida Keys and other offshore islands.

Venom: this species has a higher venom yield than any other rattlesnake. It attacks the blood cells and causes immediate and intense pain at the site of the bite, swelling and tissue damage and bleeding from the mouth: the bite is often fatal if not treated.

Subspecies: there are no subspecies.

A young eastern diamondback rattlesnake, Crotalus adamanteus.

Crotalus aquilus

Queretaran dusky rattlesnake

Note: this species was previously known as *Crotalus triseriatus aquilus* but in a recent paper Michael Dorcas raised it to a full species.[9]

Description: a small rattlesnake growing to about 60cm (24in) in length. It is brown or grey in colour, with males sometimes having a greenish or yellowish cast. The dorsal blotches are darker than the ground colour and may be roughly square or they may take the form of crossbars, especially towards the tail. The head is mainly light in colour, with a dark streak from each eye to the corner of the mouth.

Distribution (*see map*): central Mexico.

Habitat: rocky and lightly wooded places in high mountain ranges, to an altitude of over 3,000m (9,800ft).

Venom: the venom of this species appears to act mainly on the blood cells, producing localized pain and swelling. Faintness and perspiration have also been reported.

Subspecies: there are no subspecies.

9. Michael E. Dorcas, 1992, 'Relationships among montane populations of *Crotalus lepidus* and *Crotalus triseriastus*', in *Biology of the Pit Vipers*, eds. J. A. Campbell and E.D. Brodie Jr: 71–87, Selva, Tyler, Texas.

Queretaran dusky rattlesnake, Crotalus aquilus, *a recently described species, previously thought to be a form of the Mexican dusky rattlesnake. Photo by David Barker.*

Crotalus atrox

Western diamondback rattlesnake

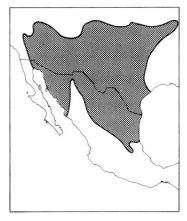

Description: a large species that routinely exceeds 1m (3ft 3in) in length and sometimes grows to over 2m (6ft 6in). It is usually greyish in colour but may also be pinkish, yellowish-grey, dull red or brick red. The diamond-shaped markings of this species are not always well defined, being slightly darker than the background colour and with their margins of pale scales often incomplete. There are often smaller dark markings along the flanks, alternating with the diamonds. There is a dark, wedge-shaped stripe from the eye to the corner of the mouth, sometimes with thin pale lines above and below it. Its tail, possibly the most distinctive feature, has four to six black and white bands of roughly equal width.

Distribution (*see map*): this species occurs almost coast to coast in the southern United States and northern Mexico, in a broad band from central southern California and Sonora to the Gulf of Mexico in Texas and north-east Mexico. It also occurs on several islands in the Gulf of California.

Habitat: dry, arid places, especially where there is scrubby vegetation, sparse grass, rocky outcrops and dry river beds. It is normally regarded as a lowland species, although it occurs at altitudes of over 2,000m (6,500ft) in the United States and in northern Mexico. It also occurs below sea-level, near the Salton Sea in California. This is one of the species often encountered on desert roads at night.

Venom: a very dangerous species, which gives a high venom yield (second only to the eastern diamondback). The venom acts mainly on the blood cells, causing intense pain, swelling, tissue damage, changes in blood pressure, nausea, etc. Serious bites are often lethal unless treated.

Western diamondback rattlesnake, Crotalus atrox, *in habitat in the Organ Pipe Cactus National Monument, southern Arizona.*

Subspecies: there are no subspecies currently recognized, although several of the rattlesnakes on islands in the Gulf of California, which are regarded as full species at the moment, are very closely related to *C. atrox*.

Crotalus basiliscus

Mexican west coast rattlesnake

Description: this large rattlesnake often grows to 1m (3ft 3in) or more and exceptionally to 2m (6ft 6in). It is brown, reddish-brown, greenish or yellowish-brown in colour and has a pattern of diamond-shaped blotches along its back, but the blotches may be only slightly darker than the background colour. Each diamond has a margin of white or yellow scales, which may be incomplete, especially towards the tail. Large specimens become ridge-backed. The head is pale in colour, but there is a dark, wedge-shaped marking from the eye to the corner of the mouth.

Distribution (*see map*): the west coast of Mexico, from southern Sonora to Michoacán, extending about 100–200km (62–124 miles) inland.

Habitat: coastal thorn scrub and deciduous forest, and pine-oak forest at higher altitudes.

Venom: this species gives a fairly large yield of venom but its effects are not known. Probably similar to that of the black-tailed rattlesnake (*C. molossus*).

Subspecies: there are no subspecies recognized at present. The form previously known as *Crotalus basiliscus oaxacus* is now considered to be a subspecies of *C. molossus*.

Mexican west coast rattlesnake, Crotalus basiliscus. *Photo by David Barker.*

Crotalus catalinensis

Santa Catalina rattleless rattlesnake

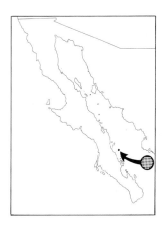

Description: a medium-sized rattlesnake, growing to about 60cm (24in), occasionally slightly longer, and with a slender build. There are two distinct colour forms. The most common is light brown or reddish-brown in colour with darker diamond-shaped blotches. Each blotch has a dark border and is outlined with light coloured scales. A wide brown stripe passes through each eye and ends at the corner of the mouth; it is bordered on each side by thinner, pale stripes. The other is ash-grey in colour, with darker grey markings. There are also pale stripes along the centre of the large scales over each eye (the supraoculars). Its most distinctive characteristic is the lack of a rattle – it usually has only one segment because the others drop off as soon as they form.

Distribution (*see map*): the island of Santa Catalina, in the Gulf of California.

Santa Catalina Island rattlesnake, Crotalus catalinensis. *This is the famous 'rattleless' rattlesnake. Photo by David Barker.*

Habitat: dry and rocky. Santa Catalina is a barren island with only cacti and scrub. It apparently climbs into low bushes in search of lizards and nestling birds.

Venom: unknown but likely to be similar to that of *Crotalus ruber*.

Subspecies: there are no subspecies. This rattlesnake may be most closely related to the red diamond rattlesnake, *Crotalus ruber*, which occurs on the adjacent peninsula of Baja California, or to the Mojave rattlesnake, *C. scutulatus*.

Crotalus cerastes

Sidewinder

Description: a medium-sized rattlesnake, growing to about 70cm (28in), and unique among rattlesnakes in that females grow larger than males. It is also the stoutest species of rattlesnake. Its colour closely matches that of the soil on which it lives and can vary from cream, through pale grey and tan to pink. The blotches along its back also vary in colour but are usually somewhat darker than the background. They are not well defined and may be oval or angular in shape, and widely spaced, with the areas between them lighter than the general background colour. There is a narrow, dark line from each eye to the angle of the mouth. The scales over the eyes (the supraoculars) are elongated, pointed and horn like, making the species readily identifiable.

Distribution (*see map*): the desert region of south-western United States and adjacent parts of Mexico. In the Gulf of California it occurs on the large island of Tiburón.

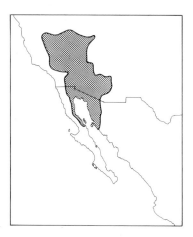

Habitat: deserts, typically among dunes but also in other sandy places. When it is found in areas of consolidated sand or gravel it is usually near sandy river beds, etc. with sparse vegetation. It moves across loose sand with a characteristic looping motion.

The sidewinder, Crotalus cerastes. Note how well camouflaged this species is.

Venom: not normally regarded as an especially dangerous species but local pain and swelling occur.

Subspecies: there are three subspecies:

- *C. cerastes cerastes* occurs in the northernmost parts of the range.

- *C. c. cercobombus* occurs in south–central Arizona and north-western Sonora.

- *C. c. laterorepens* occurs in south-eastern California, south-eastern Arizona and around the north of the Gulf of California.

The differences between these subspecies are slight.

Crotalus durissus

Neotropical rattlesnake

Description: a large, heavily built rattlesnake frequently growing to 1m (3ft 3in) or more and occasionally exceeding 1.5m (5ft) in length. Because of its huge distribution, with 14 subspecies currently recognized, a general description is almost impossible. Large specimens develop a ridge along their back, giving them an almost triangular cross-section, especially along the front third of their length. The markings consist of diamonds, which range from being well defined to amost impossible to make out. Similarly, the coloration is highly variable: they may be brown, yellow, greenish, olive, brick red, light grey, charcoal grey or almost black. Sometimes the blotches along the back are considerably darker than the background colour, or they may be a different colour altogether. At other times the colour of the blotches and the background are the same, and the pale scales that outline the diamonds are the only form of markings. This is especially so in the case of *C. d. vegrandis*, in which the white markings may lose their diamond-shaped pattern and take the form of speckles, sometimes merging into broken bands across the snake's back. Occasionally, as in the subspecies from Aruba Island (*C. d. unicolor*), the white scales are faint or absent and the snake has a more or less uniform coloration. In most individuals the markings on the neck consist of a pair of parallel lines of the same colour as the dorsal blotches, and this is perhaps the best means of identification (although, in any case, this is the only species of rattlesnake over most of its large range). There is usually a dark line across the top of the head, joining the eyes, and this continues through each eye and to the angle of the mouth.

Distribution (*see map*): from Mexico to Argentina and therefore by far the most widely distributed rattlesnake, and the only one that occurs south of Mexico. Over most of its range it is the only species of rattlesnake, but there are large gaps in its distribution, caused by unsuitable habitat. In particular, the species does not seem to occur in Panama and so the populations in Central American are isolated from those in South America. It is also absent from most of the Amazon Basin. It lives on several small islands off the coast of Venezuela.

Habitat: dry, tropical forests and grasslands. It does not live in closed canopy forests or in very damp places, which accounts for its absence from the Amazon Basin and parts of Central America. It has been found in quite small, isolated, open areas surrounded by rain forest.

Venom: the two forms about which most information is available are the Mexican and Central American subspecies, *C. d. durissus*, and the South American subspecies *C. d. terrificus*. The venoms of these two forms differ greatly in their composition and therefore their effects. That of *C. d. durissus* appears to be similar to most North American rattlesnake venoms in that it acts mainly on the blood cells, causing local pain, swelling and haemorrhaging. *C. d. terrificus* venom, on the other hand, contains elements that act on the nervous system, causing paralysis along with shock, nerve degeneration and kidney failure. There are few local effects such as pain and swelling. The mortality rate is high in cases of bites from this subspecies – up to three-quarters of victims die unless they are treated. Appropriate treatment with antivenom reduces this considerably.

Subspecies: there are 14 subspecies:

The Urocoan rattlesnake, Crotalus durissus vegrandis, *is one of the 14 subspecies of the wide-ranging neotropical rattlesnake.*

- *C. durissus cascavella* occurs in Brazil.

- *C. d. collilineatus* occurs in central Brazil and there are isolated populations in the north-east of that country.

- *C. d. culminatus* comes from south-western Mexico.

- *C. d. cumanensis* occurs in Colombia and the coastal region of Venezuela.

- *C. d. dryinas* occurs along the north coast of the Guianas and possibly inland where these countries border northern Brazil.

- *C. d. durissus* occurs along the Pacific coast of southern Mexico and much of Central America as far south as Costa Rica.

- *C. d. marajoensis* occurs only on the large island of Marajó, Brazil, at the mouth of the Amazon.

- *C. d. ruruima* occurs near the border between Venezuela and northern Brazil, near Mount Roraima, and possibly in nearby parts of Guyana.

- *C. d. terrificus* is the subspecies that occurs throughout most of the species' range in South America, i.e. from south-eastern Peru, east to the Atlantic coast of Brazil and south to northern and central Argentina, being absent only where the habitat is unsuitable or where other subspecies live.

- *C. d. totanatus* occurs in north-eastern Mexico.

- *C. d. trigonicus* occurs in south-western Guyana and perhaps in neighbouring regions.

- *C. d. tzabcan* occurs in the Yucatan Peninsula of Mexico and adjacent parts of Belize and Guatemala.

- *C. d. unicolor* occurs only on the island of Aruba, off the Venezuelan coast.

- *C. d. vegrandis* occurs in eastern Venezuela.

Note: both the last two subspecies, *C. d. unicolor* and *C. d. vegrandis*, are sometimes regarded as full species and may be found listed in other publications as *Crotalus unicolor* and *C. vegrandis*.

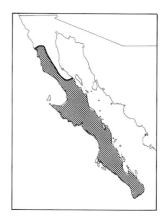

Crotalus enyo

Baja rattlesnake

Description: a small rattlesnake, averaging about 50cm (20in) in length and only occasionally growing to 80cm (31in) or slightly more. This species has a small, narrow head and a relatively large rattle. It is usually some shade of grey or brown in colour with well-defined, roundish blotches of reddish- to yellowish-brown. Each blotch has a black border. There are smaller, less clear, blotches along the flanks, in line with the main ones. The supraocular scales slant upwards to form small ridges over the eyes, but are not nearly as prominent as those of the sidewinder.

Distribution (*see map*): Baja California, including several islands in the Gulf of California, and Magdalena and Santa Margarita, off the Pacific coast.

Habitat: dry, rocky places, often where there are cacti and thorn scrub.

Venom: the effects of the venom are unknown.

Subspecies: there are three subspecies:

- *C. enyo cerralvensis* occurs on the island of Cerralvo.

- *C. e. enyo* occurs on the peninsula south of El Rosario and is also the subspecies found on the islands, except Cerralvo.

- *C. e. furvus* occurs in northern Baja, as far south as El Rosario.

The Baja, or Lower California, rattlesnake, Crotalus enyo, *is found only on the Baja California peninsula and some of its offshore islands.*

Crotalus exsul

Cedros Island rattlesnake

Description: as currently recognized, up to about 90cm (35in) in length, which is significantly smaller than its closest mainland relative, the red diamond rattlesnake (but see below). It is reddish or reddish-brown in colour, with diamond-shaped blotches outlined in white. The tail is black and white immediately in front of the rattle.

Distribution (*see map*): found only on Cedros island, off the Pacific coast of Baja California. See note below.

Habitat: rocky and barren. The island is in the path of cool, fog-laden, onshore winds at certain times of the year.

Venom: unknown but probably similar to that of *Crotalus ruber*.

Subspecies: there are no recognized subspecies.

Note: recently, several authorities have doubted that *C. exsul* is significantly different from *C. ruber*, which is found on the mainland. If they are indeed the same species, the name will be *C. exsul*, because that was the name allocated first, in 1883, nine years before the name *ruber*. This means that the subspecies that are at present in the species *C. ruber* would become *C. exsul exsul* (Cedros island and mainland California and Baja California) and *C. e. lorenzoensis* (Isla San Lorenzo). The subspecies *C. ruber lucasensis*, which is found in the Cape region of Baja California, would become *C. e. lucasensis*, although it may not be a valid subspecies either. Lee Grismer and colleagues have shown that the rattlesnakes found in the small mountain ranges of the Vizcaino Peninsula (midway between Cedros Island and the mainland of Baja California) are intermediate between the ones found on Cedros Island and those that occur elsewhere, and they suspect that the population in the south of Baja California may be merely a colour variant.[10]

Cedros Island rattlesnake, Crotalus exsul.

10. L. L. Grismer, J. A. McGuire and B. D. Hollingworth, 1994, 'A report on the herpetofauna of the Vizcaino Peninsula, Baja California, Mexico, with a discussion of its biogeographic and taxonomic implications', *Bulletin of the Southern Californian Academy of Sciences*, 93, (2): 45–80.

Crotalus horridus

Timber rattlesnake, canebrake rattlesnake

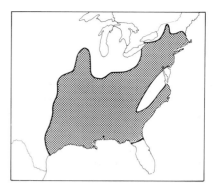

Description: a large, heavy-bodied rattlesnake, growing to 1m (3ft 3in) in length and known to grow to 1.8m (almost 6ft) under exceptional circumstances. A very distinctive species, although it can be variable in its colour and markings. The ground colour may be grey or yellowish. Over this are a number of velvety black chevrons or crossbars. The background colour becomes darker towards the tail and some forms of the timber rattlesnake, *C. h. horridus*, are heavily suffused with black, making the markings difficult to see. The canebrake rattlesnake (*C. h. atricaudatus*), has an additional marking in the form of an orange or cinnamon coloured line running the length of its back, superimposed over the black crossbands.

Distribution (*see map*): eastern and south-eastern United States, apart from peninsular Florida, where it is absent.

Habitat: the canebrake is a lowland rattlesnake that lives in well-wooded places, including swamps and river courses. In the north, the timber rattlesnake is more often asociated with rocky, hilly regions, partly because lowland populations have been eliminated through agriculture and development but also because it requires rocky outcrops in which to overwinter.

Venom: although the venom yield is less than that of the western diamondback and its potency is also slightly less, this is a dangerous species whose bite can be fatal if not treated. Symptoms include local pain and swelling, followed by nausea.

Subspecies: there are two subspecies:

- *C. horridus. atricaudatus*, the canebrake rattlesnake, occurs throughout the broad coastal belt from Virginia to central Texas.

- *C. h. horridus*, the timber rattlesnake, occurs in the north-central and north-eastern United States, almost into Canada.

The canebrake rattlesnake, Crotalus horridus atricaudatus, *occurs only in the eastern United States.*

Crotalus intermedius

Mexican small-headed rattlesnake

Description: a small rattlesnake that only rarely grows to more than 60cm (24in) in length. It is light grey or brownish-grey in colour with a series of small but well-defined, brown or reddish-brown blotches along its back. Each blotch has a thin black edge. A dark line runs from the lower part of each eye, above the angle of the jaw and on to the side of the neck. The area immediately below this stripe is often white or pale in colour.

Distribution (*see map*): southern Mexico, where there are a number of isolated populations.

Habitat: this species lives only between altitudes of 2,000 and 3,000m (6,500–9,800ft), which accounts for its patchy distribution. Within its montane habitat, it occurs mainly in humid pine-oak forest, usually near rocks. One subspecies (*intermedius*) is also found in high deserts, where it appears to be most active after heavy rain, and another (*omiltemanus*) has been collected in cloud forest.

Venom: the effects of its venom are unknown.

Subspecies: there are three subspecies:

- *C. intermedius gloydi* occurs in southern Mexico, in the state of Oaxaca.

- *C. i. intermedius* occurs furthest east, in parts of the states of Hidalgo, Veracruz and Puebla.

- *C. i. omiltemanus* occurs in the south-western state of Guerrero.

The small-headed rattlesnake, Crotalus intermedius, *is a small montane species from southern Mexico. The subspecies illustrated is* C. i. gloydi, *from the state of Oaxaca. Photo by David Barker.*

Crotalus lannomi

Autlan rattlesnake

Description: only one specimen of this species is known, found dead on the road. It measured nearly 64cm (25in) in length, of which 7cm (2¾in) made up the tail. It was stout, with a wide head and a small rattle, and grey in colour, with dark brown blotches along its back.

Distribution (*see map*): the state of Jalisco, western Mexico.

Habitat: wooded, with rocky outcrops.

Venom: unknown.

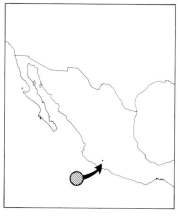

Subspecies: there are no subspecies. Its relationships with other rattlesnakes are unclear and are likely to remain so until additional specimens are found.

The Autlan rattlesnake, Crotalus lannomi, *is known from a single specimen – and this is it! It was found dead on the road in western Mexico and no further specimens have been collected. Photo by John Tashjian, courtesy of Brigham Young University, Utah.*

Crotalus lepidus

Rock rattlesnake

Description: a medium-sized rattlesnake, usually growing to about 60–70cm (24–28in), but occasionally to 80cm (31in). This species is usually very distinctive, though it varies greatly. Typically, it is grey or greenish-grey in colour, with widely spaced crossbands of black, dark brown or dark grey. Variations include snakes with brown background coloration, and others in which the crossbands are reduced to spots along the back. Some forms have additional markings, in the form of small spots or mottling between the crossbars. Almost every specimen has a bold dark stripe that runs backwards from each eye to beyond the angle of the jaw. It has a small, flat head and a relatively large rattle. A peculiarity of this species is that it shows sexual dimorphism: the background colour of females is grey or greyish-brown whereas that of males is greenish-grey.

Distribution (*see map*): from south-eastern Arizona, southern New Mexico and south-western Texas, south into north-central Mexico, where it extends well down into the Central Highlands. It occurs up to an altitude of 3,000m (9,850ft).

Habitat: rocky places, just as its name suggests. These include rock outcrops and scree slopes (talus slides) within pine-oak forests.

Venom: this species gives a fairly small yield of venom. The properties of the venom vary. It usually attacks the blood cells, causing pain, bruising and swelling at the site of the bite, but some populations from Chihuahua and parts of Arizona and New Mexico have venom that contains proteins similar to those found in the venom of the Mojave rattlesnake, which affects the nervous system. When this type of protein is present, it renders the venom from 3 to 100 times more potent than the 'normal' type. Bites from this species should, therefore, always be treated seriously, although there have been no known fatalities from it.

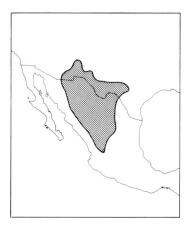

Subspecies: there are four subspecies:

- *C. lepidus klauberi*, the banded rock rattlesnake, is the subspecies found in Arizona and south-western New Mexico and north-western parts of the species' Mexican range. Its crossbands are usually well defined, often black, and the background colour is usually grey or greenish-grey.

- *C. l. lepidus* comes from south-eastern New Mexico and south-western Texas and extends well down into north-eastern Mexico. Its crossbands are often poorly defined, especially on the front half of its body.

- *C. l. maculosus* comes from the south-western parts of the species' Mexican range. This subspecies tends to be brown in colour and its body is heavily spotted with darker brown.

- *C. l. morulus* is from the southern part of the species' range in Mexico. It is also brown but the crossbars are well defined and there are few markings between them.

Overleaf: *The rock rattlesnake,* Crotalus lepidus, *is a highly variable species. The subspecies illustrated is the banded rock rattlesnake,* C. l. klauberi.

Crotalus mitchellii

Speckled rattlesnake

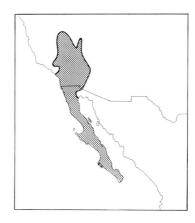

Description: a fairly large rattlesnake, normally reaching almost 1m (3ft 3in) in length. Two of the island subspecies differ from mainland forms in this aspect (see below). This species is highly variable in colour. It is typically pale grey or yellowish-grey but may also be cream, yellow, orange, pink or light brown. Similarly, its markings, which take the form of blotches on the front part of the body but widen to become crossbands towards the tail, are usually dark grey but can also be orange, reddish, brown or black. The markings are often poorly defined and some snakes have an overall 'washed out' appearance.

Distribution (*see map*): southern California, southern Nevada, western Arizona and nearly all of Baja California, including many of the Gulf islands as well as the islands of Magdalena and Santa Margarita off the Pacific coast.

Habitat: rocky places in deserts and desert foothills.

Venom: there appear to be wide differences in both the yields of venom and its potency, according to subspecies and possibly according to other factors. Symptoms appear to be mainly confined to the site of the bite.

Subspecies: there are five subspecies:

- *C. mitchellii. angelensis* lives only on the island of Angel de la Guarda, in the Gulf of California. This subspecies is significantly larger than the mainland forms, and may grow to over 1.3m (4ft 3in) in length.

- *C. m. mitchellii* occurs on the southern half of the Baja California peninsula.

- *C. m. muertensis* occurs only on the island of El Muerto, in the Gulf of· California. This subspecies is smaller than the mainland forms, with a maximum size under 70cm (28in).

- *C. m. pyrrhus* occurs in the northern half of Baja California, in southern California and western Arizona.

- *C. m. stephensi* is the most northerly subspecies, and occurs in southern Nevada and adjacent parts of southern California.

The south-western subspecies of the speckled rattlesnake, Crotalus mitchellii pyrrhus.

Crotalus molossus

Black-tailed rattlesnake

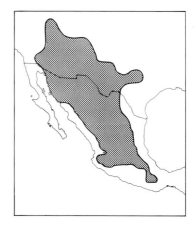

Description: a fairly large rattlesnake, growing to about 1m (3ft 3in). Its coloration varies considerably: it may be grey, olive, yellowish, rust or cream in colour, with a series of brown to black blotches along its back. The blotches are normally outlined with white, cream or pale brown scales. The characteristic marking of this species is the dark tail that gives it its common name, and many specimens from the United States also have a black 'mask' over their snout, which joins with the eye stripes to pass backwards to the corners of the mouth.

Distribution (*see map*): south-central United States (central and southern Arizona, New Mexico and south-western Texas) and much of central Mexico. The range of this species is complementary to that of *C. basiliscus* in western Mexico, and the two species hybridize where they come into contact with one another. They appear to be each other's closest relatives.

Habitat: pine-oak woods and scrubby places, often within the transition between lowland deserts and mountain ranges. They may be active during the late afternoon, especially after rain.

Venom: apparently similar to that of the western diamondback in terms of yield and potency. Fortunately, this species is normally very placid.

Subspecies: there are four subspecies:

- *C. molussus estebanensis* occurs on the island of San Esteban, in the Gulf of California. This subspecies appears to be in the process of losing its rattle, which typically has fewer segments than snakes from the mainland.

- *C. m. molossus* is the form found in the United States and in adjacent parts of northern Mexico.

- *C. m. nigrescens* occurs throughout central Mexico and on the island of Tiburón in the Gulf of California.

- *C. m. oaxacus* occurs in central Oaxaca and Puebla, Mexico. This subspecies was previously known as *C. basiliscus oaxacus.*

A typical black-tailed rattlesnake, Crotalus molossus molossus, *from south-eastern Arizona. Other subspecies lack the black 'mask' and also vary in coloration.*

Mexican lance-headed rattlesnake

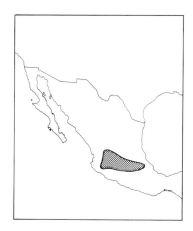

Description: a medium-sized rattlesnake, growing to about 70 or 80cm (28–31in), occasionally to 1m (3ft 3in). As its name suggests, this species has a narrow head. It has a complex and beautiful pattern. The background colour is light brown, buff, cream or tan. The markings consist of large, oval, chestnut or dark brown blotches along the back and flanks, where they interlock with one another to form a reticulated pattern. The head is also marked with rounded brown blotches, some of them elongated, and a distinctive cream stripe across the top of the preocular scales.

Distribution (*see map*): a fairly small area in south-central Mexico.

Habitat: rocky places within grassy meadows and other open areas within pine-oak forests at altitudes of about 1,500 to 2,600m (4,900–8,500ft). It apparently takes refuge in gopher burrows.

Venom: the effects of the venom of this species are unknown.

Subspecies: there are no recognized subspecies.

Mexican lance-headed rattlesnake, Crotalus polystictus, *one of the most beautiful and distinctively marked species. Photo by David Barker.*

Crotalus pricei

Twin-spotted rattlesnake

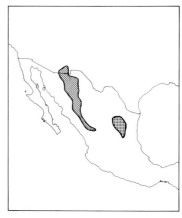

Description: a small rattlesnake of about 50cm (20in) and rarely exceeding 60cm (24in) in length. It is most commonly grey in colour but may also be brown or reddish-brown. Its markings are usually quite distinctive, consisting as they do of two parallel rows of dark blotches along the back. Occasionally, these blotches join across the mid-line to form a single row of dumbell-shaped blotches or crossbars. A dark stripe runs from the lower edge of each eye to the angle of the jaw.

Distribution (*see map*): from south-eastern Arizona (Pinaleño, Santa Rita, Chiricahua and Huachuca Mountains) down through central Mexico as far as Durango, Tamaulipas and Nuevo Leon, in suitable habitat.

Habitat: pine-oak forests. It usually occurs on south-facing scree slopes (talus slides) between 2,000 and 3,000m (6,500–9,500ft) but may also be found among rock outcrops, rocky ledges and even in grassy valleys at appropriate altitudes.

Venom: it produces very little venom, which appears to be quite mild in its effects.

Subspecies: there are two subspecies:

- *C. pricei miquihuanus* lives only in a relatively small area within the Sierra Madre Oriental (Eastern Sierra Madre), making a gap of many hundreds of kilometres between the two populations. This may be due to the inaccessibility of the intervening mountain ranges, rather than because the species is absent from them.

- *C. p. pricei* has a fairly extensive, though patchy, range from Arizona down into the Sierra Madre Occidental (Western Sierra Madre).

The twin-spotted rattlesnake, Crotalus pricei, *is a small montane species. The western subspecies,* C. p. pricei, *is illustrated. Photo by David Barker.*

Crotalus pusillus

Tancitaran dusky rattlesnake

Description: this is among the smallest species of rattlesnake, rarely growing to more than 50cm (20in). It is brownish-grey in colour with a single row of darker grey or brownish blotches down its back. The blotches are angular in shape and well separated from one another. The spaces between them are sometimes reddish-brown. The stripe from each eye to the angle of the jaw is very bold in this species and is picked out with a thinner, pale line above and below it.

Distribution (*see map*): small montane areas in southern Jalisco and west-central Michoacán, Mexico.

Habitat: clearings such as fields in pine-oak forests. It is active mostly by day due to the cold nights within its habitat.

Venom: unknown.

Subspecies: there are no subspecies.

The Tancitaran dusky rattlesnake, Crotalus pusillus, *is one of the smallest species and has a very restricted range within the mountains of western Mexico. Photo by David Barker.*

Crotalus ruber

Red diamond rattlesnake

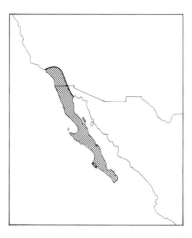

Description: a large and impressive rattlesnake, growing to over 1m (3ft 3in) in length and occasionally to 1.5m (5ft). It is typically reddish-brown or dull brick red in colour but may also be brown or olive in the southern parts of its range (subspecies *lucasensis*). Regardless of colour, the large diamonds usually have white edges, although the white scales may be absent in certain island forms. A broad reddish or brown stripe runs from the eye, backwards to the upper margin of the mouth, and it may be bordered by narrower white diagonal lines above and below. The tail has narrow black and broad white bands. In red specimens the tail contrasts especially strongly.

Distribution (*see map*): south-western California and Baja California, except for the most arid desert region at the head of the Gulf of California. It is also found on several of the islands in the Gulf of California and on the island of Santa Margarita, off the Pacific coast of Baja California.

Habitat: desert regions, especially where there is cover in the form of scrub or rocks. Often found in small rocky gullies.

Venom: thought to be similar to that of the western diamondback. This species has a reputation for being extremely placid.

Subspecies: there are three subspecies:

- *C. ruber lorenzoensis* lives only on the island of San Lorenzo Sur. This subspecies is smaller than those of the mainland and there is a tendency for the segments of its rattle to fall off. These and other differences may justify its reclassification as a full species.

- *C. r. lucasensis* (often wrongly spelled *lucansensis*) occurs in the Cape Region of Baja California, from Loreto south. It is brown or olive in colour and is said to be more aggressive than the nominate subspecies.

- *C. r. ruber* is the subspecies found in southern California and through Baja California except for the Cape Region.

Note: The classification of this species is in a state of flux.

The red diamond rattlesnake, Crotalus ruber, *is a large and impressive rattler from south-western California and Baja California.*

Crotalus scutulatus

Mojave rattlesnake

Description: a medium-sized rattlesnake that rarely grows to more than 1m (3ft 3in) in length. It is greenish, olive, brown, yellowish-brown or straw yellow in colour with angular blotches of dark olive, dark brown or black along its back. The blotches are usually well separated from one another and tend to contrast more strongly with the background colour than those of the western diamondback, a species with which it is often confused. The tail has narrow black and wide white bands, another means of distinguishing it from the western diamondback (which has tail bands of roughly equal width). The scales above the eyes are large and often have several shallow ridges running across them.

Distribution (*see map*): from the Mojave Desert in southern California and Nevada, across Arizona and down into south-central Mexico as far as Puebla and Veracruz. It also occurs in extreme south-western New Mexico and the Big Bend region of Texas.

Habitat: deserts, including sandy flats and dry hillsides. Although it is a lowland species in the north, it occurs above 2,500m (8,200ft) in the south, where it lives in rocky places.

Venom: the Mojave rattlesnake is a very dangerous species. It produces two types of venom. The more dangerous type contains powerful neurotoxins, attacking the nervous system and leading to breathing problems, paralysis and death. It is 20 times more toxic than the venom of the western diamondback, for instance. Snakes from certain populations of Mojave rattlesnakes lack this type of venom, however, and are less dangerous.

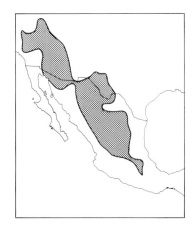

Subspecies: there are two subspecies:

- *C. scutulatus salvini* occurs in the southernmost part of the species' range, in Tlaxcala, Puebla and west-central Veracruz. This subspecies occurs in rocky areas and lava flows.

- *C. s. scutulatus* occurs in the United States and most of the species' Mexican range.

Mojare rattlesnake, Crotalus scutalatus.

Crotalus stejnegeri

Long-tailed rattlesnake

Description: a small rattlesnake, growing to about 60–70cm (24–28in), rarely longer. As its name suggests, it has a long tail and, possibly associated with this, a very small rattle. It is pale brown or fawn, with a row of brown blotches down its back. Each blotch has a bold black edge, and there are additional brown markings on the head and face.

Distribution (*see map*): a small area in the Sierra Madre Occidental, in south-western Durango and south-eastern Sinaloa, Mexico.

Habitat: pine-oak and tropical deciduous forests, between 500 and 1,200m (1,600–3,900ft) elevation. It is a very rare species, of which only about 12 specimens have been captured.

Venom: nothing is known regarding this species' venom.

Subspecies: there are no subspecies.

The long-tailed rattlesnake, Crotalus stejnegeri, *which has a small range in the mountains of central Mexico. Photo by David Barker.*

Crotalus tigris

Tiger rattlesnake

Description: a moderately large rattlesnake that normally grows to about 80cm (32in) in length. It has a small head and a large rattle. It is one of the more attractively marked species, with a ground colour of pale grey, blue-grey or pink, turning to pink or orange on the flanks. It has a series of vague crossbands along its length, which are grey or bluish-grey in colour. The head is not strongly marked, and its eyes are pink, with fine grey flecks.

Distribution (*see map*): strictly within the Sonoran Desert: south-central Arizona and much of the state of Sonora, Mexico, including the island of Tiburón in the Gulf of California.

Habitat: strongly associated with rocky mountainsides, hillsides and outcrops, usually where saguaro and other large and small cacti grow.

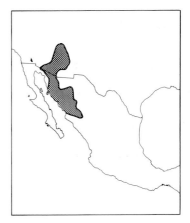

Venom: this species gives a small yield of highly potent venom, similar to that of the Mojave rattlesnake. It is, however, placid and rarely strikes without provocation.

Subspecies: there are no subspecies.

The tiger rattlesnake, Crotalus tigris, *is a handsome species from the Sonoran Desert, where it occurs exclusively in rocky places.*

Tortuga Island rattlesnake

Description: a fairly large rattler, growing to about 1m (3ft 3in) in length. It is very similar in appearance to the western diamondback, to which it is closely related. It differs mainly in having light centres to the diamond-shaped blotches along its back.

Distribution (*see map*): found only on the island of Tortuga in the Gulf of California where it occurs in very high densities.

Habitat: a barren and rocky desert island, with cacti and other drought-resistant plants.

Venom: probably similar to that of the western diamondback rattlesnake.

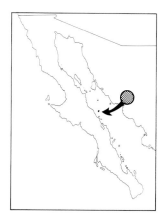

Subspecies: there are no subspecies. *C. tortugensis* is very closely related to *C. atrox*, and the differences between them appear to be slight.

The Tortuga Island rattler, Crotalus tortugensis, *is restricted to a small rocky island several miles out in the Gulf of California. Photo by David Barker.*

Crotalus transversus

Cross-banded mountain rattlesnake

Description: a very small rattlesnake, with the largest known specimen measuring only 46.5cm (18⅓in) in length. It may be orange or grey, and has a series of narrow black or brown crossbands down its back, making it unmistakable.

Distribution (*see map*): found only in a small area near Mexico City, at 2,900m (9,500ft) and above.

Habitat: cool, open forests, among volcanic rocks. Fewer than 20 specimens of this rare species have been collected.

Venom: nothing is known regarding its venom.

Subspecies: there are no subspecies.

The cross-banded mountain rattlesnake, Crotalus transversus, *a small species restricted to high elevations in central Mexico. Photo by John Tashjian, courtesy of Charles Radcliffe.*

Crotalus triseriatus

Mexican dusky rattlesnake

Description: a fairly small rattlesnake, growing to 60–70cm (24–28in). A highly variable species that may be grey, brown or orange in colour, or any shade between these. A series of blotches runs along its back, and these may be outlined in black or white, but sometimes they are poorly defined. An additional row of spots runs along each flank, roughly opposite the ones on the centre of the back. There is a bold dark stripe running from the lower portion of the eye to the angle of the jaw.

Distribution (*see map*): south-central Mexico.

Habitat: mountains, in rocky, grassy clearings in pine-oak forest, often near streams. It has been found as high as 4,572m (15,000ft) – the highest recorded altitude for any rattlesnake (or any other snake in the New World).

Venom: nothing is known regarding this species' venom.

Subspecies: there are two subspecies:

• *C. triseriatus armstrongi* occupies the eastern portions of the species' range. This subspecies is dimorphic in colour: females are brown or greyish whereas males have a greenish or yellowish cast.

• *C. t. triseriatus* occupies the western portion of the species' range.

Note: the subspecies previously known as *C. t. aquilus* is treated as a separate species, *Crotalus aquilus*.

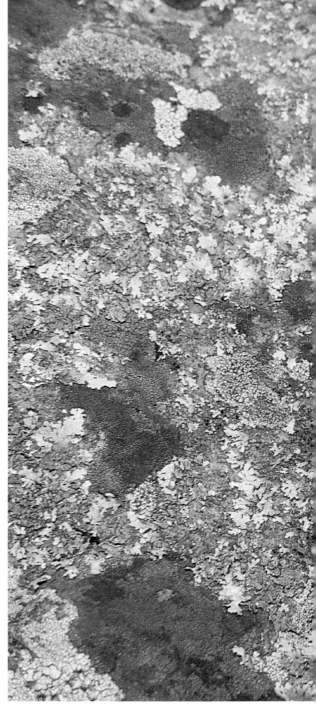

Mexican dusky rattlesnake, Crotalus triseriatus. *The subspecies* C. t. armstrongi *is shown. Photo by David Barker.*

Crotalus viridis

Western rattlesnake

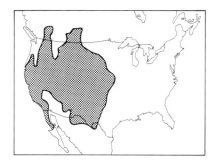

Description: some subspecies of this rattlesnake grow large, to over 1m (3ft 3in) in length, whereas others remain comparatively small, rarely growing longer than about 70 to 80cm (28–31in). Because of the great amount of variation between subspecies, colours and markings are given below.

Distribution (*see map*): from Canada (extreme southern British Columbia, Alberta and Saskatchewan) in the north through most of western and central United States and into northern Mexico (Baja California in the west and Chihuahua and Coahuila in the east).

Habitat: found in a variety of different habitats, including coastal dunes, prairies, desert foothills, mountain forests and rocky outcrops. Not all subspecies have such a wide range of habitats, however. The northern subspecies, for instance, are more commonly found on prairies and may hibernate in communal dens among rock outcrops.

Venom: the various subspecies have different yields and venom characteristics. Although this species produces venom in significantly smaller quantities than the western diamondback, bites can be serious. They typically produce pain and swelling at the site of the bite. However, bites from snakes from at least some populations have also produced symptoms associated with neurotoxins, such as twitching,

The western rattlesnake is divided into a number of subspecies. This is a young specimen of the Great Basin subspecies, Crotalus viridis lutosus.

breathing difficulties and paralysis. The midget faded rattlesnake (*C. v. concolor*), from Utah and Colorado, in particular, seems to produce a far more toxic venom, weight for weight, than the other forms, and its characteristics are similar to those of the Mojave rattlesnake (*C. scutulatus*).

Subspecies: there are nine subspecies:

- *C. viridis abyssus* is the Grand Canyon rattlesnake, found only in northern Arizona. It is reddish in colour with poorly defined blotches along its back.

- *C. v. caliginus* lives only on the island of Coronado del Sur, off the Pacific coast of Baja California. It is a small subspecies.

- *C. v. cerberus* is the Arizona black rattlesnake, confined mostly to Arizona but extending into a small area of extreme western New Mexico. This subspecies is very dark in colour and the markings are sometimes obscured. Otherwise, it is dark grey, with black or dark brown blotches, separated by narrow white lines between them.

- *C. v. concolor* is the midget faded rattlesnake, found on either side of the border between Utah and Colorado. It is cream, tan or yellowish above, and its oval blotches are only slightly darker than the background. It is the smallest subspecies, growing to about 60cm (24in) in length.

- *C. v. helleri* is the southern Pacific rattlesnake, found along a narrow coastal belt from southern California and into the northern half of Baja California. This subspecies has dark blotches of grey, greenish-grey or black, contrasting strongly with the background colour, which is light grey or brownish-grey.

- *C. v. lutosus* is the Great Basin rattlesnake, found in northern Nevada and adjacent parts of surrounding states. Its background colour is pale, often light brown, buff or tan, with bold, medium to dark brown blotches, widely separated from one another and edged in black.

- *C. v. nuntius* is the Hopi rattlesnake, found in north-eastern Arizona. It is buff, pale brown or

The southern Pacific rattlesnake, Crotalus viridis helleri, *of which this a young specimen, is the form that occurs in southern California and northwestern Mexico.*

tan, with medium brown blotches that are edged with black and surrounded by a thin white border. This is a dwarf subspecies, rarely growing to more than 60cm (24in).

- *C. v. oreganus* is the northern Pacific rattlesnake, found throughout most of northern California and Oregon and into Washington and British Columbia, Canada. This subspecies is similar to *C. v. helleri* but is usually darker, with bold rings around its tail.

- *C. v. viridis* is the prairie rattlesnake, found from extreme southern Alberta and Saskatchewan, through the central United States and into extreme northern Mexico. It is brown or grey in colour and often has an overall greenish tinge. The blotches along its back are brown, well defined and outlined with a very narrow white line.

Crotalus willardi

Ridge-nosed rattlesnake

Description: a small rattlesnake, growing to about 50cm (20in), with occasional specimens over 60cm (24in). This pretty species is immediately recognizable by the shape of its head, and the markings on its face and those on its body, which are unlike those of any other species of rattlesnake. The feature from which it gets its name is a sharp ridge running forward from each eye to the snout, caused by the upturning of the edges of the scales in that region. Two bold lines, usually of pure white, run along the side of the face. Depending on subspecies, the upper one may start at the tip of the snout or behind the eye. Below this line is a wide area, usually of chestnut brown, then another white line, following roughly the line of the mouth. The background colour of the body is usually rust brown but may be greyish. There is a row of large, square-shaped blotches along the centre of the back, darker in colour than the background and edged front and back with black or dark brown. The narrow spaces between the blotches are lighter in colour than the rest of the snake, so that they appear to form short crossbars along its length.

Distribution (*see map*): extreme south-eastern Arizona (Huachuca and Santa Rita Mountains) and south-western New Mexico (Animas Mountains) into mountain ranges of north-eastern Mexico and south along the Sierra Madre Occidental as far as south-western Zacatecas.

Habitat: pine-oak woods from 1,600 to 2,750m (5,250–9,000ft) elevation. Within this habitat, they appear to favour grassy places and moist and humid microhabitats along canyon bottoms.

Venom: poorly known but thought to be mild.

Subspecies: there are five subspecies:

- *C. willardi amabilis*, the Del Nido ridge-nosed rattlesnake, is from the Sierra del Nido in northern Chihuahua, Mexico.

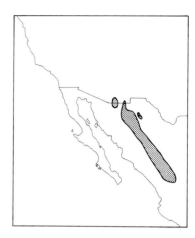

- *C. w. meridionalis*, the southern ridge-nosed rattlesnake, occurs in mountain ranges in the Mexican states of Durango and Zacatecas.

- *C. w. obscurus*, the New Mexico ridge-nosed rattlesnake, lives in the Animas and Peloncillo Mountains in New Mexico.

- *C. w. silus*, the West Chihuahua ridge-nosed rattlesnake, occurs in mountain ranges in north-eastern Sonora and western Chihuahua.

- *C. w. willardi*, the Arizona ridge-nosed rattlesnake, occurs in the Huachuca, Patagonia and Santa Rita Mountains of south-eastern Arizona and in mountain ranges in northern Sonora, Mexico.

Note: differences between the subspecies are slight and they are distinguished mainly by variations in the facial markings or in the numbers of ventral and subcaudal scales (or, more easily, by locality).

The ridge-nosed, or Willard's, rattlesnake, Crotalus willardi, is a small, attractive and distinctively marked species that is found in the mountains of Arizona, New Mexico and northern Mexico. The subspecies shown is one of the less common ones, C. w. amabilis. Photo by David Barker.

Genus *Sistrurus*, massassauga and pygmy rattlesnakes

Three species of small rattlesnakes belong to the genus *Sistrurus*. One species is found only in Mexico, another is found only in the south-eastern United States, while the third occurs mainly in the United States but strays just over the border into northern Mexico. They differ from other rattlesnakes (*Crotalus*) in having nine large plates on the top of their heads, like the harmless snakes such as ratsnakes and kingsnakes, etc. They also have very small rattles that are capable of producing only a faint, buzzing sound when vibrated, more like that of an insect than a rattlesnake. Although they are small, the three species in this genus can give painful bites, producing a variety of symptoms.

Sistrurus catenatus

Massassauga

Description: a small rattlesnake that usually grows to about 50cm (20in) but may occasionally approach 1m (3ft 3in), making it the largest member of the genus. It is pale brown or grey in colour, with a series of well-separated, dark or chestnut brown blotches along its back. There is a pair of elongated brown blotches on its neck and a dark line running from the snout, across each eye and obliquely down to the angle of the jaw. Below this dark line is a thinner pale one. Massassaugas from some northern areas are sometimes heavily suffused with black pigment (melanistic).

Distribution (*see map*): from southern Ontario, Canada, diagonally down through the central United States to Texas, New Mexico and extreme south-eastern Arizona, occurring just over the border in adjacent parts of northern Mexico. There are two isolated populations in the Mexican states of Nuevo León and Cohuila.

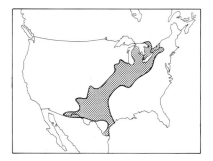

Habitat: it is found in a variety of habitats. In the north it seems to prefer damp, swampy places, at least for part of the year, whereas in Arizona, New Mexico and Texas it occurs in desert grassland.

Venom: this species gives a small yield of very toxic venom, acting on both the blood cells and the nervous system. Symptoms include pain and swelling at the site of the bite, and nausea.

Subspecies: there are three subspecies:

• *S. catenatus catenatus*, the eastern massassauga, comes from the north-eastern parts of the species' range. The eastern massassauga prefers damp meadows, swamps and bogs but also it lives in drier situations. The adults tend to become darker than other subspecies, and are sometimes completely black.

- *S. c. edwardsi*, the desert massassauga, is smaller and more slender than other subspecies. It occurs in the more southern, drier parts of the species' range, and includes the Mexican populations.

- *S. c. tergeminus*, the western massassauga, occurs in the central United States, down into Texas and to the Gulf of Mexico. It is paler than the eastern massassauga.

Massassauga, Sistrurus catenatus. *The specimen shown is melanistic, and probably comes from a population towards the north of the species' range.*

Sistrurus miliarius

Pygmy rattlesnake

Description: this small rattlesnake grows to about 50cm (20in) but occasionally it reaches 70cm (28in). It is pale grey, grey or reddish in colour, with a row of small, rounded, dark grey blotches along the centre of its back. These blotches may interrupt a narrow pink, orange or cinnamon stripe that runs along the mid line and extends on to the top of the head. There are more blotches, often smaller and less well defined, on the flanks. The tail is slender and relatively long and the rattle is minute.

Distribution (*see map*): central and south-eastern United States.

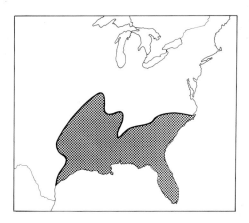

Habitat: pine woods, pine-oak woods and palmetto scrub, usually near water. It often shelters under leaf-litter, bark and other debris during the day.

Venom: although their venom is fairly toxic, pygmy rattlesnakes produce very small yields. Furthermore, their fangs are short and cannot penetrate deeply into human tissue. Most bites result in fairly minor superficial pain and swelling, but there are records of more serious symptoms.

Subspecies: there are three subspecies:

- *S. miliarius barbouri*, the dusky pygmy rattlesnake, is stippled with fine grey specks over the whole of its head and body. It occurs throughout Florida, in southern Georgia and Alabama and extreme south-eastern Mississippi.

The dusky pygmy rattlesnake, Sistrurus miliarius barbouri, *is the form of pygmy rattler found in Florida and adjoining parts of neighbouring states. Note the minuscule rattle, which produces a faint buzzing sound.*

- *S. m. miliarius*, the Carolina pygmy rattlesnake, may be grey, brown or reddish in colour, with sharp-edged blotches. It occurs in North and South Carolina and in central Georgia and Alabama.

- *S. m. streckeri*, the western pygmy rattlesnake, has a pale grey or cream coloration and small, bar-shaped, dorsal blotches. The red or orange stripe down the back of the western pygmy rattlesnake is often quite prominent.

Sistrurus ravus

Mexican pygmy rattlesnake

Description: a small species of rattlesnake, growing to about 50cm (20in) and occasionally to 75cm (30in). It is usually brown or grey in colour, with dark brown or rust blotches along its back. These blotches have narrow black edges and they usually become paler towards their centres. The colour between the blotches may also be a shade or two paler than that on the flanks. There are no stripes on the head, which is unmarked, but there is a pair of elongated blotches on the neck.

Distribution (*see map*): isolated populations occur in the highlands of southern Mexico.

Habitat: it usually lives in meadows and grassy forest clearings, especially among pine-oak forest, cloud forest and scrub. It can also be found, less frequently, in rocky places and lava beds, among cacti and other desert vegetation.

Venom: the effects of the venom of this species are unknown.

Subspecies: there are three subspecies:

- *S. ravus brunneus* comes from the Oaxacan highlands.

- *S. r. exiguus* occurs in the Sierra Madre del Sur, in the state of Guerrero.

- *S. r. ravus* occupies the largest range, in the Central Highlands south of Mexico City.

Note: The differences between the subspecies appear to be slight. Other subspecies have been described but their validity is doubtful.

The Mexican pygmy rattlesnake, Sistrurus ravus, *is the least known of the three* Sistrurus *species. Photo by David Barker.*

FURTHER READING

Among the wealth of literature on rattlesnakes, two authors stand out as representing the extremes of the popular–scientific spectrum. These are Carl Kauffeld, whose two books, *Snakes and Snake Hunting* and *Snakes: the Keeper and the Kept*, describe his adventures and observations while searching for rattlesnakes in the wild, and Laurence Klauber, whose monumental book *Rattlesnakes* summarizes his prodigious research, undertaken over many years of collecting and analysing information on rattlesnakes. These books (now unfortunately out of print) are compulsive reading for anyone who has an affinity for, and an interest in, rattlesnakes. Of the others, Jonathan Campbell and Bill Lamar's *The Venomous Reptiles of Latin America* and *The Biology of the Pit Vipers*, edited by Jonathan Campbell and Edmund Brodie, are important books that have brought our scientific knowledge of rattlesnakes (and similar snakes) into the 1990s.

Full details of these and a few other books that might be of interest are given below. References to smaller articles and papers are given throughout as footnotes.

Armstrong, Barry L. and Murphy, James B., 1979, *The Natural History of Mexican Rattlesnakes*, University of Kansas Museum of Natural History, special publication number 5.

Campbell, Jonathan A. and Brodie, Edmund D. (editors), 1992, *The Biology of the Pit Vipers*, Selva, Tyler, Texas.

Campbell, Jonathan A. and Lamar, William W., 1989, *The Venomous Reptiles of Latin America*, Cornell University Press, Ithaca, New York.

Ernst, Carl H., 1992, *Venomous Reptiles of North America*, Smithsonian Institution Press, Washington.

Kauffeld, Carl, 1957, *Snakes and Snake Hunting*, Hanover House, Garden City, N.Y.

Kauffeld, Carl, 1969, *Snakes: the Keeper and the Kept*, Doubleday and Company, Garden City, N.Y.

Klauber, Laurence M., 1972, *Rattlesnakes, Their Habits, Life Histories and Influence on Mankind* (second edition), University of California Press, Berkeley. (Klauber lists 168 pages of references, and this only included material written before 1972!)

Lowe, Charles H., Schwalbe, Cecil R. and Johnson, Terry B., 1986, *The Venomous Reptiles of Arizona*, Arizona Fish and Game Department, Phoenix.

Russell, Findlay E., 1983, *Snake Venom Poisoning*, Scolium International, New York.

INDEX

Page numbers in *italic* refer to illustrations